Bibliographic information published by the German National Library:

The German National Library lists this publication in the National Bibliography; detailed bibliographic data are available on the Internet at http://dnb.dnb.de .

Imprint:

Copyright © 2015 GRIN Verlag
Print and binding: Books on Demand GmbH, Norderstedt Germany
ISBN: 9783668771277

Aidan Mc Carron

The Impact of Advanced Automation and the Cloud on Employment

GRIN Verlag

GRIN - Your knowledge has value

Since its foundation in 1998, GRIN has specialized in publishing academic texts by students, college teachers and other academics as e-book and printed book. The website www.grin.com is an ideal platform for presenting term papers, final papers, scientific essays, dissertations and specialist books.

Visit us on the internet:

http://www.grin.com/

http://www.facebook.com/grincom

http://www.twitter.com/grin_com

The Impact of Advanced Automation and the Cloud on Employment

Aidan Mc Carron

A dissertation submitted to the University of Dublin

in partial fulfillment of the requirements for the degree of

MSc in Management of information Systems

1st *September 2015*

Acknowledgements

I would like to express my sincere gratitude to my supervisor Diana Wilson for her invaluable support, guidance and encouragement throughout the process of completing this dissertation.

I would also like to thank all of the people who took part in this research. I am grateful for the time they took to participate and the information that they provided. Without them, this dissertation would not have been possible.

Finally, I owe my deepest gratitude to my wife Emer for all of her constructive comments, patience and support given to me during this research, and to whom I dedicate this dissertation.

Abstract

One of the primary fears in the current global community is the exponential growth and continued sophistication of artificial intelligence. Fundamental to this concern is the wide-ranging impact that this growth will not only leave on the world as we currently know it, but on the place of humans in that world. This has become termed as 'the singularity'—the point in time when machines will become self-learning, and more importantly, self-aware. It is at this point that machines and robotics will be elevated from the current monotonous job operations to more high skilled areas. This study looks into the drive towards advanced automation and the increased sophistication of artificial intelligence in conjunction with the cloud and how this growth will eventually lead to technological unemployment. Some economists are predicting up to a 50% job loss or more. Predicting the future typically means extrapolating the past. It often fails to anticipate breakthroughs. But it is precisely those unpredictable breakthroughs in computing that could have the biggest impact on the workforce. Education and up skilling current workers will be the only way to ensure continued relevance within an automated workforce. By focusing on education it will ensure people are best placed to take advantage of this new age of advanced automation. This dissertation concludes that innovation through creativity will ensure employment opportunities continue to present themselves to those best prepared for such changes.

Table of Contents

List of Figures and Diagrams

1. INTRODUCTION

This thesis examines the sustained rise of advanced automation within a global context, and its impact on technological employment and society in general. As Managing Director of a cloud infrastructure company, this subject is of significant relevance to the development of the IT industry. The advent of artificial general intelligence, as defined by 'the singularity', is of fundamental importance to this study in assessing its influence on advanced automation. The following section presents a brief overview of contemporary views on this topic, as a means of highlighting the need for further research in this area.

1.1 Background and Context

The recent global recession (2007-2008) brought about a vast reduction in employment in all industries around the globe. According to International Labour organization (ILO) estimates, unemployment levels increased from 178 million in 2007 to 197 million in 2012, with a peak of 212 million reached in 2009 (Aridas, Pasquali 2013). However, global unemployment in 2013 still remains at 202 million, with a projected unemployment growth to 211 million by 2017 (see Figure 1) — even with most countries now out of recession and seeing a GDP (gross domestic product) growth (ILO, 2013). The red line illustrates the unemployment percentage during this time, while the orange level shows the worse possible projection going forward:

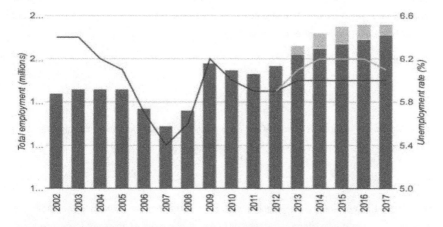

FIGURE 1: Global unemployment trends and projections

This continued growth of unemployment through a new wave of prosperity is considered by those such as Brynjolfsson, McAfee, and Manning, as the reason behind many employers' decisions to replace human employees with more cost effective automated robotic solutions, rather than any current economic climate (Brynjolfsson and McAfee, 2011; MGI, 2011; Manning 2013) — a contributing factor in ensuring unemployment continues to rise through a more stable economic setting. This, coupled with the eventuality of the 'singularity' (the moment in time when robots become self-aware and self-learning), has led to doomsday predictions from leading economists and global IT figures envisaging up to a 47% job loss or more by 2034 (Frey and Osborne, 2013).

Edward E. Leamer, director of the UCLA Anderson Forecast, states:

> If you have nothing to offer the job market that cannot be supplied better and cheaper by robots, far-away foreigners, recent immigrants or microprocessors, expect it to be exceedingly difficult to find the job to which you aspire, and plan on doing low-wage service work at the end of a long and painful road of diminished aspirations, no matter what your diploma may suggest (Semuls, 2010).

Conversely, previous technological leaps have shown this statement to be inaccurate. One example of this may be seen in retail employment numbers in the US, whereby 10% of the country's population worked in retail in 1995. Since then, the Internet has completely changed the face of retail as we know it, and the manner in which purchasing is now done. In 2012 the percentage of the population working in retail increased to 12.7% (Bureau of labor Statistics). This development demonstrates the positive effect of technology on employment in its ability to create jobs, rather than destroy jobs.

1.2 Research Question

The primary research question posed by this dissertation is:

> Will the drive towards advanced automation and the increased sophistication of artificial intelligence eventually lead to technological unemployment?

1.3 Value of Research

Employment and work-status are crucial aspects of social identity in situating people's role and purpose within the existential framework of life. While work enables us to secure basic necessities such as food, accommodation and clothing, its inherent value has a deeper historical and philsophical significance. We gain stimulation from work, and experience a wide range of emotions: exhilaration, exuberance, joy, regret, anger and despair (Holbeche and Springett, 2004). The fabric of society would change irrevocably should employment no longer exist. Artificial intelligence would dominate every aspect of civilisation, and leave us with little engagement or sense of place. However, great technological leaps have been encountered in the past.

The communications–energy mix of the First Industrial Revolution involved the printing press, the rise of coal and the steam engine. The Second Industrial Revolution was fuelled by telegraphy, telephony and oil. Now in the midst of the Third Industrial Revolution, economist and activist Jeremy Rifkin argues that the next transformation will be based on the interaction between the Internet and large-scale renewable energy production. It too will entail not only economic changes, but also profound social and philosophical revolutions (Rifkin, 2011). Nevertheless, none of the previous changes have resulted in widespread job loss. Job creation simply evolved with the changing environment into more creative means. In furthering the investigation into understanding previous technological leaps, this thesis will provide a more comprehensive assessment of the future impact of the singularity on employment.

1.4 Scope and Boundaries of this Study

This study investigates if automation is driving unemployment, and whether employment will continue to grow as the sophistication of artifical intelligence continues. The primary focus will be on the predicted timeline of the singularity, and the ramifications on employment, based on previous technological breakthroughs.

1.5 Chapter Roadmap

- Chapter 1
  This introductory chapter provides a summary of the context and relevance of the research question.

- Chapter 2
  The literature review examines: current scholarship related to the singularity, its timelines, and its predicted impact on employment; previous technlogical leaps and

their influence on employment; the growth of automation; and the current global destruction of jobs through the growth of artificial intelligence.

- Chapter 3

  Here, an overview of the various methodological approaches available for this study are presented. The reasons behind the chosen methodology for this research project will be explained. The limitations and strengths of the research project will also be discussed.

- Chapter 4

  This chapter assesses the manner in which the data colllected in the study was analysed and interpreted in a rigorous manner. The resultant findings determine the impact on employment due to the growth of automation and the singulairty.

- Chapter 5

  The concluding chapter puts forward the findings and conculsions derived from the research, thus demonstrating that the research question has been answered fully. The strengths and limitations of the research will also be highlighted, and areas of further investigation will be proposed.

2. LITERATURE REVIEW

2.1 Introduction

This chapter outlines the body of extant literature relating to the growth of artificial intelligence and its continuing place of importance within modern day society. Fundamental to this field of research is the eventuality of the 'singularity', and its inherent impact on employment. In order to provide a comprehensive assessment of the writings on this subject, it is necessary to first define 'the singularity'. A series of hypotheses regarding the projected timeline for the singularity will follow, leading to a discussion on the impact of automation on employment, and the role of the cloud within this development. The information gleaned from this review demonstrates the need for further research in this area.

2.2 Sources

The library of Trinity College, Dublin has served as the primary source of research for this dissertation. A variety of databases have been consulted throughout. These include: Academic search complete; ISI Web of Knowledge; JSTOR; and Stella search. Further papers were identified through Google Scholar, as well as web-based online articles, which were sourced via Internet search engines.

2.3 The Cloud and Advanced Automation

We are now looking into a new age that could prove the 'luddite fallacy' as being incorrect — the age of cloud computing. Cloud computing is one of the most important technological advances over the last decade, and has the potential to revolutionise the delivery of IT services to consumers (Brynjolfsson and Jordan, 2010). Cloud computing has changed the face of global business, data storage, information sharing and how we now work. It is no longer necessary for smaller businesses to maintain their own server environment in-house. Marston and Li propose that the use of the Cloud 'dramatically reduces the upfront costs of computing that deter many organisations from deploying many cutting-edge IT services' (Marston, Li et al., 2011).

One major driver for the adoption of cloud computing in SMEs is the reduction in costs and operational overheads associated with the support and maintenance of internal company-owned IT infrastructure and services (Chen, Lin 2012; Sultan, 2011; ENISA 2009). However, by reducing those costs by the removal of in-house IT services and effectively outsourcing

5

their internal IT departments to 'the cloud', companies no longer have employment, or require a drastically reduced workforce for existing IT works within their organisations. This is one of the most fundamentally overlooked points when it comes to the promotion of Cloud computing within organisations by the IT staff that cloud adoption will potentially replace. If a business no longer has work for their internal IT staff, then why would the need for the staff that implemented the solution remain?

According to the EU's Small Business Act (SBA), Ireland's SME sector lost 15% of its total workforce between 2007 and 2010, which also coincides with 79% of all Irish SMEs now using some form of cloud computing services in their organization; this jumps to 84% if you include email (Carcary et al, 2014). The challenge for IT leaders is to reduce their spending on sustaining the business, and invest more in innovative ways that drive business growth and support strategic business goals (Gartner, 2006).

The cloud is the enabler for the drive by industry, in convergence with advanced automation, to allow for increased improvements in the automation of both high and low skilled jobs. Advanced automation in IT technology is also leading to the deployment of production management functions in off-site data centres for use by multiple manufacturing sites. Examples include *Starbucks*, who are doubling the number of Clover coffeebrewing machines in operation, which connect to the cloud and track customer preferences. This technology allows recipes to be digitally updated, and help staffers remotely monitor a coffee maker's performance (Kharif 2013). *Starbucks* also plan to use connected fridges that indicate when a carton of milk has spoiled for real-time stock control (Kharif 2013).

2.3.1 Data Centre and the Cloud
A data centre is defined by Gartner as:

> The department in an enterprise that houses and maintains back-end information technology (IT) systems and data stores — its mainframes, servers and databases. In the days of large, centralized IT operations, this department and all the systems resided in one physical place, hence the name data center (Gartner, 2013).

Data centres play a key role in the delivery of cloud services. Cloud service providers use data centres to house cloud services and cloud-based resources. For cloud-hosting purposes, vendors also often own multiple data centres in several geographic locations to safeguard data availability during outages and other data centre failures. Data centres are continually being built by cloud service providers such as Facebook, Google and Microsoft to ensure increased speed by placing their facility geographically closer to their end users. By being physically closer to their end users, cloud providers can ensure usability is in real time to remove any need for physical infrastructure in the office place. 'As cloud becomes a significant enabler, enterprises are getting out of the datacentre business in droves,' says Tim Crawford, CIO strategic advisor at AVOA. 'But datacentres are not dying; Cloud is just enabling more enterprises to use third-party IT services' (Venkatraman, 2014).

2.4 Technological Unemployment

The convergence of cloud and advanced automation is believed to be a contributor to 'technological unemployment' — the term used in the push of labour from automated to non-automated industries. In 2014 Pew Research canvassed 1,896 technology professionals and economists, and found a split of opinion: 48 % of respondents believed that new technologies would displace more jobs than they would create by the year 2025, while 52 % maintained that they would not do so (Smith, Aaron, Anderson and Janna, 2014).

According to Say's law, technological unemployment is only ever temporay. Named after French economist Jean-Baptiste Say (1767-1832), the law argues that supply creates its own demand. This mechanism exists in the economic system, and guarantees the automatic reabsoption of any technologically-displaced labour (Luas, 1978). Gregory Woirol considers four major theoretical arguments that technological change could lead to net rise in unemployment as follows (Woirol, 1996):

- That there may be a lack of markets for the increased output.
- That there be a lack of capital to employ released labour.
- That the rise in purchasing power from technological change hypothesized by the Say's law compensation theory would not occur.
- That technological change led to constantly decreasing ratio of circulating to fixed capital.

2.5 Impact of Automation on Employment

Frey and Osborne postulate that '47% of all jobs could be automated in the next 20 years' (Frey, Osborne 2013). 'This wave of technological disruption to the job market has only just started' (*The Economist,* 2014). Andrew McAfee, from MIT, observes that 'automation in the manufacturing industry is a net job destroyer' (Zeilzer, 2013). From statements such as these, the subject of current technological growth appears to invite an air of caution within mainstream media, with such doomsday headlines as: 'The Machines are Going to Steal our jobs' (Worstall, 2014); and 'Robots on the Rise: Is your job at Risk?' (Goodkind, 2013). However, in order to understand the future effects of automation and the rise of the singularity, it is necessary to look back at the influence of previous advancements on both employment opportunities and job growth. From the Luddites onwards, this has proven to be a continuous ongoing challenge to employment.

The Luddites were a group of English textile workers engaged in the violent breaking up of machines from 1811 onwards (Palmer, 1998). Such vandalisation was premised by the fear of new machines taking their jobs and livelihoods. Against the backdrop of the economic hardship following the Napoleonic wars, new automated looms meant clothing could be made with fewer lower-skilled workers. As the new machines were more productive, some workers lost their relatively highly paid jobs as a result. A 'Luddite' named after the mythical English folk hero Ned "King" Ludd, is a term used (usually pejoratively) to describe people who oppose the introduction of new technology, while the 'Luddite fallacy' is the simple observation that new technology does not lead to higher overall unemployment in the economy (Ford, 2009).

It is argued that new technology does not destroy jobs – it only changes the composition of jobs in the economy (Ford, 2009). However, with the continued sophistication and growth of artificial intelligence, and in time the progressive reliance we place on automation, we could now potentially be at the tipping-point of the Luddite fallacy. Martin Ford asserts that 'if we automate even more, the economy cannot absorb the newly unemployed due to automation in other sectors, and hence it would reduce the purchasing power of the people' (Ford, 2009). Whether it can now continue to live up to the fact that new technology does not destroy jobs remains to be seen. Since 2001, with the aid of computers, telecommunication advances, and ever more efficient plant operations, U.S manufacturing productivity, or the amount of goods or services a worker produces in an hour, has increased by 24% (Huether, 2006).

In 1924 American Congress passed a resolution asking the secretary of labour to draw up a list of labour-saving devices (Bureau of Labour statistics, 1924-26), and a parallel estimate of the number of people who had been left unemployed as a result of their use. General consensus believed that the central result concerning the introduction of machinery was the reduction of total labour requirements. From this, it was assumed that all saved labour would be the total amount of unemployment. Notwithstanding, this line of reason did not match up to reality, as productivity in the United States more than quadrupled from 1870 to 2000. The study fails to take into account displaced labour as it focuses more on job growth during this particular epoch.

The same labour input produced over four times as much value in good and services, yet employment increased over six times, from 10 million to over 65 million. This can be accounted for by the increase in population during this period. However, it fails to acknowledge that population increased by six times, and productivity increased by only four times, even with the assistance of improved and more advanced technology.

It was also shown that most of the jobs held by workers in industries such as car manufacturing, which required the building of roads thus creating additional US jobs, would not have existed if it were not for advanced technology (Buckingham, 1962). Germany stands as a model example of the benefits of automation through robotics. From 1998 onwards, the German government invested in advanced manufacturing and sophisticated automation. Resultantly, trade deficit was reversed into a large surplus due to the introduction of over a million robots in the manufacturing industry, leading to the creation of close to three million jobs (Gorle, 2011).

Once of the most comprehensive reports to date on the impact of automation on employment is, 'The Impacts of Automation on Employment, 1963-2000, Final Report' (Leontief and Duchin, 1984). This effort resulted in the development of a detailed model of the probable effects of automation on the demand for labour services in fifty-three occupations. According to this model, the intensive use of automation over the next twenty years will make it possible to conserve about 10 % of the labour that would have been required to produce the same bills of goods in the absence of increased automation. Consequently, the direct displacement of production workers by specific items of automated equipment will, at least in the initial stages, be offset by increased investment demand for capital goods, thus ensuring production workers can be expected to maintain their share of the labour force.

Leontief and Duchin explain that:

> The impacts are specific to different types of work and will involve a significant increase in professionals as a proportion of the labour force and a steep decline in the relative number of clerical workers. Production workers can be expected to maintain their share of the labour force. Computations that assume the full utilisation of the projected future labour force suggest that personal and government consumption will be able to increase about 2% a year in real terms through the 1980s and between 0:5 and 1.1% through the 1990s due to the adoption of computer-based automation (in the absence of other structural changes). Whether or not the

smooth transition from the old to the newer technology can actually be realised will depend to a large extent on whether the necessary-changes in the skill structure of the labour force and its distribution between different sectors of the economy (and geographic locations) can be effectively carried but. This study projects the direction and magnitude of these changes in the structure of the-labour force and of the educational and training efforts needed to carry them out (Leontief and Duchin,1984).

The findings of this report have since been proven to be incorrect, with the lost manufacturing work being completely removed rather than displaced. The increase demand for capital goods has been offset by cheaper credit (Federal Reserve, 2001), allowing even low income families to drive consumer demand. This has been cited as a primary reason for the ecomomic crash in 2007 (International Monetary Fund Report, 2009).

This report demostrates that, according to historical changes to automation, more jobs are created on average, even with increased automation, and the labour force is simply moving towards a better educated and more creative workforce. Brynjolfsson and McAfee reinforce this idea by arguing that 'acquiring an excellent education is the best way to not be left behind as technology races ahead; motivated students and modern technologies are a formidable combination' (Brynjolfsson and McAfee, 2011). This is illustrated in Figure 2, which reveals the increased importance in Ireland of advanced education, and the clear upward growth curve of people in higher education from the economic collapse in 2008 to 2013 (Statistics from the International Labour Organisation).

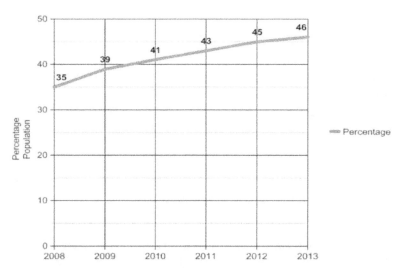

FIGURE 2: Adult Population with Advanced Education in Ireland (International Labour Organisation 2014)

The most recent ILO estimates show that the world in 2008 had a labour force of 3.1 billion — nearly 2.1 billion more than that of 1980. The growth of the world's labour force has been decelerating since 1980: while the average annual growth rate was 2.1 % in the period spanning 1980-1990, it dropped to 1.6% during 1990-2000, and then to 1.5 % from 2000-2007 (Ghose et al., 2008). This clearly suggests that even though the population is expanding, the rate of job growth is continuing to drop, as advanced automation becomes more commonplace in supplanting not only minimal physical tasks, but more advanced skilled intellectual labour also.

David Autor, an economist at MIT who has studied the connections between jobs and technology, disagrees with the possibilities that technology could account for such an abrupt change in total employment. Whilst acknowledging 'a great sag in employment beginning in 2000', the author claims 'something did change', but 'no one knows the cause.' Computer technologies are undoubtedly changing the types of jobs currently available, and those changes 'are not always for the good.' Autor notes that since the 1980s, computers have increasingly taken over such tasks as bookkeeping, clerical work, and repetitive production jobs in manufacturing — all of which typically provided middle-class pay. At the same time, higher-paying jobs requiring creativity and problem-solving skills, often aided by computers, have proliferated (Rotman, 2013). This has been confirmed by a 2014 joint report from Deloitte, the Big Four accountancy firm, and the University of Oxford (Tovey 2014), as seen in Figure 3:

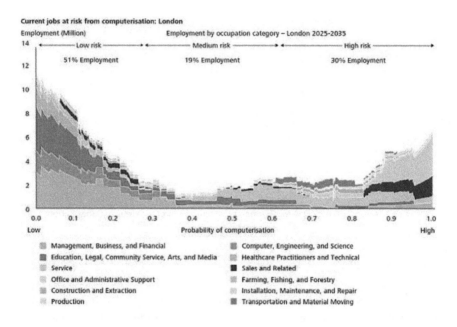

Current jobs at risk from computerisation: London

Employment (Million)   Employment by occupation category – London 2025-2035

FIGURE 3: High skilled jobs currently at risk from advanced automation (Deloitte 2014)

McAfee (2011) concurs with these statistics, stating that 'new technologies are encroaching into human skills in a way that is completely unprecedented'. Many middle-class jobs are right in the bull's-eye; even relatively high-skill work in education, medicine, and law is affected. 'The top and bottom are clearly getting farther apart.' While technology might be only one factor, says McAfee, it has been an 'underappreciated' one, and it is likely to become increasingly significant.

According to the latest figures from U.S. Bureau of Labour Statistics (BLS), they expect IT jobs to grow by 22% by 2020 due to an increased demand for software developers in the Health IT and Mobile network sectors, as shown in Figure 4:

Job growth forecast					
JOB TITLE	MAY 2010 EMPLOYMENT	2020 JOBS FORECAST	JOB GROWTH FORECAST	PCT JOB GROWTH FORECAST	EXPECTED GROWTH RATE THRU 2020
Computer support specialists	607,100	717,100	110,000	18%	About average
Software developers, applications	520,800	664,500	143,700	28%	Faster than average
Computer systems analyst	544,400	664,800	120,400	22%	Faster than average
Software developers, systems software	392,300	519,400	127,100	32%	Much faster than average
Network & computer system admins	347,300	443,800	96,500	28%	Faster than average
Computer programmers	363,100	406,800	43,700	12%	Average
Information Security Analysts, Web Developers, and Computer Network Architects	302,300	367,900	65,600	22%	Faster than average
Computer & information systems managers	307,900	363,700	55,800	18%	About average
Database administrators	110,800	144,800	34,000	31%	Much faster than average

FIGURE 4: Job growth IT sector 2010 – 2020, U.S. Bureau of Labor Statistics

Ron Hira, an associate professor of public policy at the Rochester Institute of Technology, argues that the BLS IT forecasts have been wildly wrong in the past. He claims that 'volatile occupations tend to be subject to bad forecasts, and it's clear that computer occupation employment levels are very hard to forecast' (Thibodeau, 2012). 'The forecasts are biased toward the most recent history in the occupation'. Hira places more stock in growth projections for a predictable profession, citing primary school teachers as an example. There, he conjectures that the BLS can estimate the number of births during the decade, and factor in teacher-student ratios to reach an estimate of employment growth.

The BLS has 'no methodology to estimate technological disruptions that can increase demand for computer occupations,' states Hira, listing the rapid increases in the use of the Internet and ERP systems as examples of IT disruptions that cannot be measured (Thibodeau, 2012). David Foote, CEO of Foote partners an IT labour research firm, agrees with Hira in light of 'current market volatility and uncertainty, which is unprecedented,' that anyone who makes a 10-year IT employment projection 'is kidding themselves' (Thibodeau, 2012). While there is ongoing disagreement about the driving forces behind the persistently high unemployment rates, a number of scholars have pointed at computer-controlled equipment as a possible explanation for recent jobless growth (Brynjolfsson and McAfee, 2011).

2.5.1 Outsourcing Vs. Automation

Traditionally, and pre-automation, the fear for job loss was through outsourcing to less affluent but well educated work forces in India, Poland, and China. However, the growth of artificial intelligence and the increasing sophistication of automation is now becoming a major disruption in even low cost economies, with Yahoo laying off 400 employees in its Indian office (Lunden, 2014), IBM cutting 2,000 Jobs (Rai, 2014), and Cisco also reducing its head count in these regions. With labour still being cheap in these countries, and with these companies not moving the employment to other countries, it becomes obvious that automation is not just impacting high cost first-world countries, but it is now having a real affect on low-cost societies. A 2012 report by HFS Research suggests that, 'robotic automation has the potential to wreak some dramatic, painful changes on the Indian outsourcers who are the current bulwark of the industry' (Slaby, 2012).

Discussions on the topic of automation are becoming much more common in the technology industry. According to Mark Muro, technology jobs in Asia have the potential to be on the chopping block. The economist at Brookings goes on to say that 'technology is another platform putting another pressure on developing countries' (Neal, 2014). He proposes that 'cheap labour isn't as cheap as it was', and companies are seeing that automated replacements are getting to be 'good enough' (Neal, 2014). On the other hand, not every IT or business process is suitable for automation. James Slaby from HFS research remarks that 'a business process requiring human perception, or nuanced human judgement based on years of experience is less suitable', 'which, of course, is a good thing for those of us humans who still want to contribute valuable work to our employers' (Slaby, 2012).

A recent Oxfam report shows that 85 people alone now command as much wealth as the poorest half of the world (Oxfam, 2014). This concentration of wealth is being expedited due to the unprecedented growth of wealth amongst the privileged few, who, by allowing automation to reduce employment whilst still increasing the rate of production, allow the owners and facilitators of advanced automation to increase their wealth at a more rapid pace than previously seen in history. The prosperity that has been unleashed by the digital revolution has transferred overwhelmingly to the owners of capital, and the highest-skilled workers (Ford, 2009). Nonetheless, even the employment of high skilled workers is now at risk, once the singularity arrives.

Over the past three decades, labour's share of output has shrunk globally from 64% to 59%. Meanwhile, the share of income going to the top 1% in America has risen from 9% in the 1970s to 22% today (Sharon, 2014). Unemployment has reached alarming levels in much of the first world, and not just for cyclical reasons, or due to the recent recession. In 2000 65% of working-age Americans were in employment; since then, the proportion has fallen, during good years as well as bad, to the current level of 59%. 'The wealth of the 1% richest people in the world amounts to $110tn (£60.88tn), or 65 times as much as the poorest half of the world' (Oxfam, 2014). Both they, and their corporations, are building robots that will have the net effect of letting them keep even more of that capital concentrated in their hands (Frey et Al).

Even though much of the research so far has focused on the possibility that technology could increasingly replace human labour, thus displacing jobs and creating unemployment, it has become clear due to the historical progression of technology that this is not always the case. This sort of thinking is textbook Luddism relying on a 'lump-of-labor' fallacy — the idea that there is a fixed amount of work to be done. The counter argument to a finite supply of work comes from economist Milton Friedman who claims that 'human wants and needs are infinite, which means there is always more to do' (Fridman, 2004). The argument is simple: human beings have a nature which causes them to have infinite desires. Therefore, as technology advances and satisfies our current desires, we will just move on to new wants and needs (Friedman, 2004). While it is certainly true that technological change displaces current work and jobs, it is equally true, and important, that the other result of each such change is a step-function increase in consumer standards of living. As consumers, we never resist technology change and advancements that provide us with better products and services, even at the cost of jobs (Higbie, 2014).

2.6 What is the Singularity?

Famed mathematician John Von Neumann (1903-1957) first coined 'the singularity' during a conversation with Stainislaw Ulam (1909-1984), a renowned mathematician in his own right. The term describes the point in time when Neumann believed technology would become self-aware, and exceed human intellectual capacity and control. Two of the most noted proponents of this concept are Ray Kurzweil, currently director of engineering at Google, and Vernor Vinge, a former professor of mathematics at San Diego State University. Kurzweil believes the singulairty to occur around 2045 (Kurzweil, 2005), whereas Vinge proposes an earlier timeframe of 2023. By then 'we will have the technological means to create superhuman intelligence' (Vinge, 1993). According to Stephen Hawking 'computers are likely to overtake humans in intelligence at some point in the next hundred years' (ABC, 2006). The advances in both the computer software and hardware necessary for artificial intelligence, along with research in genetics, and nanotechnology, are leading towards a technological singularity in which the intelligence of machines will outperform human intelligence. Therefore, the common held belief is not a matter of 'if' it will happen, but rather a matter of 'when'.

According to István S. N. Berkeley, the field of artificial intelligence is the 'study of man-made machines or computers which exhibit some form of human intelligence' (Berkeley, 1997). The world became more aware of the singularity and the true growth of artificial intelligence in 1997 when IBM's deep blue mainframe beat world champion, Garry Kasparov — considered the greatest chess player of all time (Barden, 2008; IBM, 1997). With the facility to process 200 Million positions per second, it soon became apparent that the ability of computers to match, and eventually supersede the ability of humans both mentally and physically, was possible.

Estimates of general rates of technological progress are always imprecise, but it is fair to say that, in the past, progress came about more slowly. The historian Henry Brooks Adams (1838-1918), determined technological progress by the power generated from coal, and estimated that power output doubled every ten years between 1840 and 1900 — a compounded rate of progress of about 7% per year (Adams, 1946). By contrast, the speed of progress today comes about at a far more rapid pace than Adams could have ever predicted. When we look at the numbers for information storage density in computer memory between 1960 and 2003, those densities increased by a factor of five million, at times progressing at a rate of 60% per year. At the same time, and according to Moore's Law, semiconductor technology has been progressing at a 40% rate for more than fifty years. These rates of progress are the catalyst for the creation of intelligent machines, from robots to automobiles to drones, which will soon dominate the global economy and in the process, drive down the intrinsic value of human labour over the coming decades.

Research fellow Eliezer Yudkowsky, from the Singularity Institute for Artificial Intelligence, California, views the singularity in three more distinct schools of thought, rather than as a single definable process. The first, 'accelerating change', is based on existing knowledge, which allows us to easily see and predict the current technological rate of change very precisely. The second, 'event horizon', centers on Vernor Vinge's superhuman intelligence break-though, which would make the future very unpredictable to forecast. Finally, the third, 'intelligence explosion', refers to the situation in which humans in partnership with machines would increase the speed of human intelligence exponentially, whilst not overtaking human imagination and control (Yudkowsky, 2007).

2.7 Projected Timeline for the Singularity

A number of prominent researchers in this field (Good, 1965; Solomonoff, 1985; Vinge, 1993; Moravec, 1999; Kurzweil 2005; Sandberg, 2009; Baum and Goertzel, 2010; and Chalmers, 2010) have argued that at some point in this century humanity will develop artificial intelligence programs capable of substituting human performance in almost every field, including artificial intelligence research. This will greatly accelerate technological progress as AIs design their successors. Dr Stuart Armstrong (Oxford University) conducted a study of Artificial General Intelligence (AGI) predictions as part of the 2012 Singularity Summit. He found the median predication to be 2040, and concluded that: 'It's not fully formalised, but my current 80% estimate is something like five to one hundred years' (Armstrong, 2012). AI Singularity theory has its roots and its projected timeline firmly aligned within Moore's Law. Moore's Law states 'the obervation that steady technological improvments in miniaturisation leads to a doubling of the density of transistors on new integrated circuits every 18 months' (Moore, 1965).

In 1951 mathematician, Alan Turing, theorised about the idea of machines becoming more intelligent than humans. He developed what became known as the 'Turing Test'. In this test, one person sits at a computer terminal; at the other end sits another person and an AI program. The operator at the terminal is not aware of the identity of the computer or the person, and asks a series of questions in order to ascertain which is the AI and which is the human. Turing said that if the operator were unable to differentiate, then the AI would be a successful equivalent to human intelligence (Turing, 1950). To this date no AI has passed the Turing Test, as of January 2015.

The projected timeline for the singularity contains a common set of components, which form the framework for expert predictions on this area. These include:

- *Moore's Law*
- *Storage*
- *Supercomputers*

The following sections analyses these components in more detail, and examines their progress and evolutionary contributions to the establishment of this framework.

2.7.1 Moore's Law

In his 1965 paper entitled, 'Cramming more components onto integrated circuits', Gordon Moore put forward the idea that 'the obervation that steady technological improvments in miniaturisation leads to a doubling of the density of transistors on new integrated circuits every 18 months' (Moore, 1965, p.4). Due to the accurate nature of this prediction, this became known as 'Moore's law', which is used to describe a long-term trend in the history of computing hardware. The number of transistors that can be placed inexpensively on an integrated circuit doubles approximately every two years. This trend has continued in a smooth and predictable curve for over half a century, and is expected to endure beyond 2020 (Moore, 1965). The capabilities of many electronic devices are strongly linked to Moore's law. These include: processing speed, memory capacity, sensors and even the pixels in digital cameras. These processes are improving at exponential rates as shown in Figure 5. This is dramatically enhancing the impact of digital electronics in nearly every segment of the world economy, and functions as a cornerstone to the predicted timeline of the singularity.

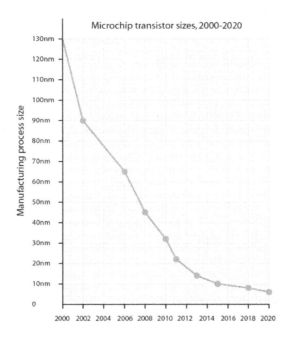

FIGURE 5: Moore's Law versus Transistor sizes 2000-2020

2.7.2 Storage

Data storage has progressed at an ever-increasing rate over the last fifty years, and will continue to do so for the foreseeable future. Trends have consistently shown exponential growth in this area, with home PCs with 100 GB hard drives common by 2005, and 1 terabyte (TB) hard drives common by 2010. This increase will continue to allow for the cheaper storage of more complex and detailed information. It will also allow for the increased deployment and usage of cloud-based data storage. Highly regarded computer architect Jeff Hawkins proposes:

> Let's say the cortex has 32 trillion synapses. If we represented each synapse using only two bits and each byte has eight bits, then we would need roughly 8 trillion bytes of memory as a human cortex. So we would need about eighty modern hard drives to have the same amount of memory as a human cortex (Hawkins, 2004).

However, this would not allow for human intelligence as described by Alfred Binet as 'judgment, otherwise called "good sense," "practical sense," "initiative," the faculty of adapting one's self to circumstances and auto-critique' (Binet, 1905). Therefore, the ability to build an artificial brain with the same capacity as humans is very much within reach of existing technology.

Figure 6 shows the continued upward growth of storage capacity. The graph displays a clear upward trend where storage capacity increases, stablises, then advances again. The graph also shows rampant growth since 2000 than shown in the previous 20 years with continued acceleration.

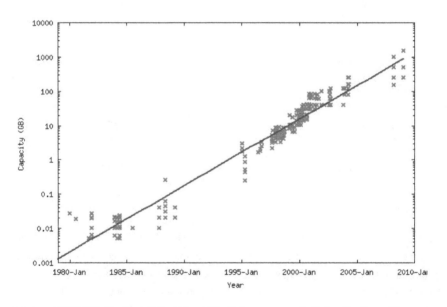

FIGURE 6: Continued upward growth of storage capacity (futuretimeline.net)

2.7.3 Supercomputers

Supercomputers are very large groups of computers that work together, combining their abilities to perform tasks that individual desktop computers would simply not have the power nor the compute ability to process. A supercomputer is typically used for scientific and engineering applications that must handle very large databases, or do a great amount of computation (or both). These include highly intensive calculations such as problems involving quantum mechanics, weather forecasting, climate research, astronomy, molecular modeling, and physical simulations (such as simulation of airplanes in wind tunnels, simulation of nuclear weapons detonations and research into nuclear fusion).

Since October 2010 China has been home to the world's fastest supercomputer. The *Tianhe-1A* supercomputer, located at the National Supercomputing Center in Tianjin, is capable of 2.5 petaFLOPS — that is, over 2½ quadrillion (two and a half thousand million million) floating-point operations per second (IBM 210). For decades, the growth of supercomputer power has followed a remarkably smooth and predictable trend, as seen in Figure 7. If this trend of rapid improvement continues, it is likely that complete simulations of the human brain, and all of its neurons will be possible by 2025 (Kurzweil, 2005).

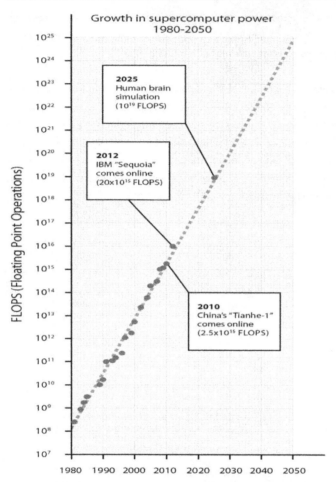

FIGURE 7: Growth in Supercomputer Power 1980-2050 (futuretimeline.net)

Experts in this field of analysis, such as Kurzweil, Vinge et al (1990,1993), use these details to predict the timeline of the singularity. Despite recent forecasting work on individual AI-related aspects of the world, such as the future cost of computing power (Anderson et al. 2002); the development of computer chess players (Kurzweil 1990); and the economic impact of robotic systems that substitute for human labour (Peláez and Kyriakou 2008), there currently lacks a unified single approach to determine when this might happen.

2.8 Conclusion

The growth of the cloud, advanced automation and the eventuality of the singularity, and its impact to employment have been debated since the 1800s. Although there is a large amount of material available on this subject, the majority of the views tend to be based on external factors being used as a framework to best guess when the singularity will become reality. There are clear indications from the reviewed material that global employment patterns are changing. IT, alongside the increased use of robotics, advanced automation and the cloud, is having a real and profound affect on this development. However, it remains to be discovered if this is the case, as the reviewed material has shown similar patterns of employment change before artificial intelligence and computer software became as dominant, in the form of advanced automation as we see today.

The eventuality of the singularity demonstrates a clear indication that job growth, sustained employment, and ongoing job creation is going to be a formidable challenge for all industries in the coming years and decades.

3. RESEARCH METHODOLOGY

3.1 Introduction

Before any concrete examination of the influences of advanced automation and cloud computing on employment can begin, it is necessary to first define the chosen methodological model upon which this study is built. This chapter discusses the research design that was chosen for this project. It also explains the following considerations that were taken into account when choosing the research philosophy: the approach and strategy employed to conduct the primary research; the manner in which the research was conducted; and the data collected.

3.2 Purpose of Research

A research methodology is a structured framework used to describe, explain and justify the various methods for conducting research (Saunders, Lewis, & Thornhill, 2009). The purpose of this research study is to assess the impact that the growth and increased use of advanced automation, and its integration with the cloud, will have on future employment opportunities. It is hoped that this research will provide insight into what we can expect in terms of real world impacts from such a situation, and how best to engage with this issue going forward. Such scholarship will also illuminate further revelations into how IT workers are going to be most affected by these changes.

3.3 Research Philosophy

Saunders, Lewis et al., (2009) define 'research' as 'the systematic collection and interpretation of information with a clear purpose, to find things out.' Research can be broadly divided into two categories: quantitative research, and qualitative research. Punch (2005) presents a simplified yet clear definition for both:

> Quantitative research is empirical research where the data is in the form of numbers. Qualitative research is empirical research where the data is not in the form of numbers.

Creswell describes research as a process of steps used to collect and analyse information that increases our understanding of a topic or issue (Creswell, 2002).

This research project embraces a two-tiered methodological approach in which quantitative and qualitative elements are married through the ideologies of Saunders, Lewis et al., —

24

pragmatism, positivism, realism, and interpretivism. Each school of thought will be critiqued in order to select the most appropriate ideology best suited to this course of research.

3.3.1 Pragmatism

Through pragmatism the researcher adapts both objective and subjective points of view. Results may be taken from either observed facts or subjective viewpoints. Pragmatism rejects positivism, on the grounds that no theory can satisfy its demands, and rejects interpretivism because practically any theory would satisfy them (Pansiri, 2005). Pragmatism looks to use both qualitative and quantitative research methods to allow for a better understanding of the social phenomena. By using both subjective and objective viewpoints, when collecting and understanding the data, the researcher is permitted to select methods appropriate in the investigation of the research question. 'The pragmatic approach to science involves using the method which appears best suited to the research problem and not getting caught up in philosophical debates about which is the best approach' (Moksha, 2013).

3.3.2 Positivism

The natural world has, typically, been measured and modeled utilising a positivist philosophy. Myers (Mingers and Willcocks, 2005) states that:

> The basic ontological assumption of positivist philosophy is that reality is objectively given and can be described by measurable properties that are independent of the observer (researcher) and his or her instruments.

In terms of methodology, truth in positivist inquiry is achieved through the verification and replication of observable findings (Guba and Lincoln, 2005).

This philosophical position is characterised by hypothesis testing, derived from present theory. It postulates that knowledge is only valid based on observations of external reality. This position is based on values of reason, and is focused mainly on facts obtained from experience or direct observation, which are empirically measured by means of quantitative methods, such as surveys and experiments, as well as the belief that the development of theoretical models can be generalised (Flowers, 2009). Positivism is not always suitable for social science where there is a need to interpret deeper meaning in discourse that is represented in a collection of observed behaviours and activities (Guest, Namey and Mitchell, 2013). Positivists therefore, emphasise the use of valid and reliable methods in order to describe and explain the events. A research is positivist if there is evidence of formal propositions.

3.3.3 Realism

Realism shares some philosophical principles with positivism and adopts a similar, natural-sciences approach to the development of knowledge. The researcher is biased by existing experience and results are ideally based upon the facts observed that can be understood and confirmed. 'The philosophy of realism is that there is a reality quite independent of the mind' (Saunders, Lewis et al., 2009).

There are currently two types of realism – 'Direct' and 'Critical'. Direct realism is where our senses portray the world as it is, and we perceive objects as they are. 'Through the use of appropriate methods, reality can be understood' (Bryman and Bell, 2011). Critical realism argues that the researcher's conceptualization of reality is just a way of knowing 'that reality', and that there is a distinction between the object and the terms used to describe and understand that object. In this way, critical realism complements positivism. Bhaskar (2010) says of critical realism that;

> It provides a set of perspectives on society (and nature) and on how to understand them. It is not a substitute for, but rather helps to guide, empirically controlled investigations into the structures generating social phenomena.

The objective of realism is to generate a reasonable approximation of reality close to the subject that is being observed. Realists take a scientific approach to the collection, analysis and development of data, but view their findings as evidence-based probabilities (Saunders, Lewis et al. 2009, Guest, Namey and Mitchell 2013).

Jeff Easton notes that critical realism is particularly well suited as a companion to case research. It justifies the study of any situation regardless of the number of research units involved, but only if the process involves thoughtful, in depth research, with the objective of understanding why things are as they are (Easton, 2010, p. 119). This thesis employs critical realism in its use of a case study to investigate the use of advanced automation in a cloud provider.

3.3.4 Interpretivism

Interpretivism is in direct contrast to Positivism in relation to the collection, analysis and interpretation of data. Walsham (2009) describes interpretivism as:

> Interpretive methods of research start from the position that our knowledge of reality, including the domain of human action, is a social construction by human factors and that this applies equally to researchers. Thus, there is no objective reality that can be discovered by researchers and replicated by others, in contrast to the assumptions of positivist science. Intepretivism is thus an epistemological position, concerned with approaches to the understanding of reality and asserting that all such knowledge is necessarily a social construction, and thus subjective (Walsham, 2009).

One of the basic ideas of interpretivism regarding the individual is that all human action is meaningful, and hence 'has to be interpreted and understood within the context of social practices' (Scott et al., 1996). As interpretivism leans towards the collection of qualitative data, and uses methods such as unstructured interviews, this philosophy was deemed not suitable for this research.

3.4 Research Strategy

Several strategies were looked at for this research; with a number of secondary data sources identified to backup up conclusions combined with primary data from the survey. Pragmatism and critical realism are the chosen methodological framework for this research, as they provide a mixed methods approach with both qualitative and quantitative data collection, and analysis techniques.

This investigation into the impact of advanced automation and the cloud on technological employment will be carried through two strategies:

1. An online survey of technology professionals to understand whether advanced automation is acknowledged in the current work environment, and the impact such automation might have on employment in the IT sector going forward.

2. A Case study of my existing company Dediserve will also be used as a real world example of a current IT company utilising automation to reduce head count and drive efficiency in order to increase growth and primarily profit.

3.4.1 Online Survey

An online survey was selected as a primary method for collection of the primary data for this research. Nesbary (2000) defines survey research as the process of collecting representative sample data from a larger population, and using the sample to infer attributes of the population. The main purpose of a survey is to estimate, with significant precision, the percentage of population that has a specific attribute, by collecting data from a small portion of the total population (Wallen & Fraenkel, 2001).

According to Groves et al., (2004), surveys have the following characteristics:

- Information is gathered primarily by asking questions.
- Information is collected from only a subset of the population, described as a sample rather than all its members.

The most common method of survey is a questionnaire, where sets of questions are given to a sample set and the answers are interpreted (figure 8):

FIGURE 8: Survey Response Process, Groves et Al (2004)

This method was chosen as it contains the following features:

- Faster, simpler and cheaper.
- Respondents have adequate time to think through their answers.
- Respondents who are not easily approachable, can also be reached.
- Very accurate and less bias.

Online surveys provide a more efficient and cost effective way to generate a large number of responses in a relatively short period of time, and have a substantial cost advantage over other methods of data collection (Wright, 2005). However, the data gathered in this fashion has a number of limitations:

- Answers may vary due to random mouse clicks or first options shown. This is of particular concern for longer surveys where the participant risks becoming bored.

- There is no option for follow-up questions based on the respondent's answer selection.

- It is possible that the survey link that was sent to the intended recipients is passed on to people not qualified to answer, which might skew results.

These limitations will be taken into account when analysing the survey results.

The questions in the survey aim to cover four distinct but related topics; these areas include questions on the advanced automation, cloud services, employment and the singularity. Although these are four distinct sub-topics, they combine to provide a more clear and comprehensive overview of the understanding of the synergies between each sub-topic, allowing for a clearer picture of the interlining commonalities between them and their combined shared impacts.

3.4.2 Data Collection

This section details the process involved in the collection of the primary data for this research. This survey was developed after a detailed literature review in Chapter 2 which focused the information query on more relevant issues to the topic, and allowed for a more succinct line of questioning from IT professionals regarding their opinions on the stated topic. The survey comprises twenty-two questions, which are split into four sections. Section A covers 'advanced automation', section B 'cloud services', section C 'data centre' and section D 'employment'. Combined, these provide a rounded more comprehensive view of the participants' understanding of advanced automation, its growth, and its affect on employment going forward.

3.4.3 Case Study

Becker (1970) explains that a case study refers to a detailed analysis of an individual case supposing that 'one can properly acquire knowledge of the phenomenon from intensive exploration of a single case'. As the case study is the study of the processes and use of automation of a single company, it will not be the primary focus of this research because the case study only offers insight into a single particular situation, rather than a sweeping overview of the impact of automation and the growth of artificial intelligence in the IT sector.

The chosen case study for this research project will be used as a real-world example, in combination with the survey replies, to give a more rounded view of the following: current obstacles; the impact of automation and cloud services on the employment of contemporary IT professionals, and the resulting long term issues that may appear in the sector. Researcher Robert K. Yin defines the case study research method as an empirical inquiry that investigates a contemporary phenomenon within its real-life context; when the boundaries between phenomenon and context are not clearly evident; and in which multiple sources of evidence are used (Yin, 1984).

Yin looks at six distinct steps that can be used for the collection of data for a case study:

- Determine and define the research questions.
- Select the cases and determine data gathering and analysis techniques.
- Prepare to collect the data.
- Collect data in the field.
- Evaluate and analyse the data.
- Prepare the report.

The results of the case study will be more opinion-based that statistical. The focus of this thesis's case study will be on a single IT company and their use of advanced automation.

3.5 Survey Tool

The survey tool chosen for this research project is an online tool called *SurveyMonkey*. This was selected due to the in-depth level of functionality provided by this web-based tool. It afforded a wide range of choice including check boxes, multi select boxes, as well as the ability to add text boxes for open-ended questions, and an exit survey option, which presented an easy exit point at any stage of the survey to participants who did not wish to submit data. This tool was also picked for its ability to provide clear and concise reporting tools on the collected data.

3.6 Participant Demographic

As this survey examines the impact of the ongoing advancement of automation and artificial intelligence on employment in the IT sector primarily, this survey will be aimed at people who currently work in technical roles within the IT sector. The participants will be chosen from both personal *LinkedIn* connections (1000+), and *Twitter* followers (900+) of which approximately 95% work in the IT sector or in technical roles.

3.7 Conclusions

This chapter outlined a selection of methodological approaches available for this research, including their limitations and advantages. Target subjects for this study were any IT professionals working in the IT industry. The research method chosen was that of pragmatism with the use of a survey and case study as a research strategy. The following chapter presents the findings and analysis of this study.

4. FINDINGS AND ANALYSIS

4.1 Introduction

This chapter details the manner in which the quantitative and qualitative survey data was collected and analysed. The resultant findings, alongside the case study, will test previously discussed hypotheses, and provide answers to the research question, and sub-questions, posed in Chapter 3. In order to begin such an examination, it is necessary to first provide a description of the response rate and data analysis. This is followed by a detailed report of the survey findings.

4.2 Data Analysis

The data was gathered online via the online survey tool, *SurveyMonkey*. Once collected, it was exported to *excel* (XLS), and comma-separated values (CSV) files for further analysis. Due to the large array of unique answers garnered from question 15, responses were separated into three categories: 1) irrelevant; 2) intuitive knowledge; 3) and accurate knowledge. The three categories were selected based on what a data centre was, according to the official definition defined by Gartner. The respondents, who provided some knowledge, and those who choose to skip or provide a wholly inaccurate statement, were also recorded. This allowed for more transparent visual representation of the replies to this question.

4.3 Survey Results

The survey was broken across four segments that included: 1) advanced automation; 2) cloud services; 3) data centre; 4) and employment in IT. Each question allowed for multiple-choice options — with question 15 providing a text box to allow for the recording of the respondents' personal opinions. The link to the survey was distributed to colleagues, and posted to groups on *LinkedIn*, that consistent of IT professionals only. A target sample population of 100 respondents was expected, and 111 responses were received. The survey was open for four weeks, from 1 May 2015 to 31 May 2015.

Each of the 111 survey respondents provided full permission for publication of their results, as outlined in the information sheet provided at the start of the survey in accordance with the ethical approval application submitted to Trinity College, Dublin.

4.3.1 Advanced Automation
This section presents the data acquired from questions 2-8 of the survey.

Questions 2 asks: Do you believe advanced automation will have a positive or negative impact on employment overall? The results are as follows:

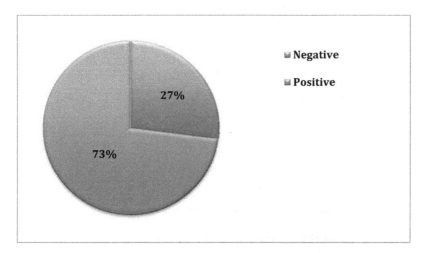

FIGURE 9: Will advanced automation have a positive or negative impact on employment?

The majority of respondents, 73%, believe that advanced automation would have a positive impact on employment going forward, while 27% disagreed. This was confirmed by a Metra Martech report delivered in 2011, It concluded that they had determined a job-creation ratio of 3.6 jobs for every robot deployed, and that with more robots, fewer jobs are lost. That's why Germany, with hourly rates almost 50% higher than in the US, has remained globally competitive: they have twice as many robots per 10,000 workers as do Americans (Martech 2011)

Question 3 asks: Do you believe advanced automation should be feared or embraced? The results are as follows:

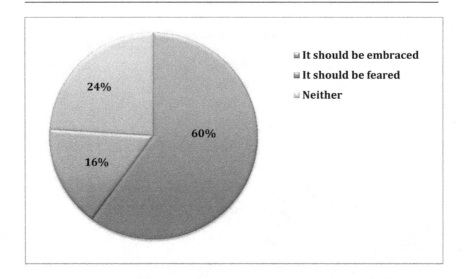

24%

16%

60%

- It should be embraced
- It should be feared
- Neither

FIGURE 10: Should automaton be feared or embraced?

A near two-thirds majority of 60% believe we should be embracing advanced automation, whilst 16% state it should be feared, and 24% believe neither statement applies. The belief that it should be embraced corresponds with a recent Grant Thornton International Business Report, which surveyed 2,571 executives in 36 economies, with the majority of firms, 56%, now planning to automate operations and practices (Thornton, 2015).

Question 4 asks: Do you believe advanced automation will have a positive or negative impact on employment in the IT sector? The results are as follows:

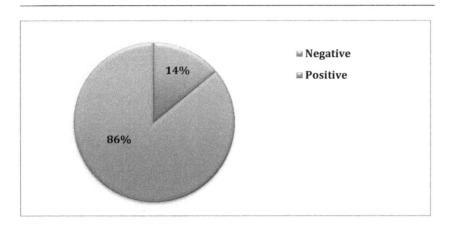

FIGURE 11: Will automation affect employment in the IT sector?

When asked if advanced automation would have a positive impact on employment, a surprisingly large majority of 86% believes it will have a positive effect.

Question 5 asks: Do you believe advanced automation will become intelligent enough to fully replace high skilled jobs in the next 10 to 20 years, such as surgery, accountancy, or flight control? The results are as follows:

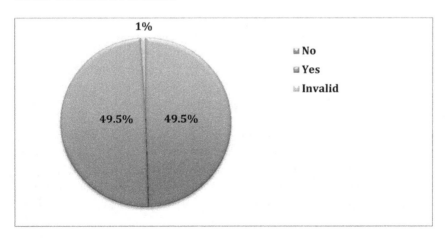

FIGURE 12: Do you believe advanced automation will replace skilled jobs?

50% of the respondents to question 5 answered 'yes' to whether advanced automation will replace high skilled jobs, with the same percentage saying 'no'. One respondent skipped the question completely. Our study has shown high skilled jobs are ripe for disruption including medicine with IBM's super computer, Watson, already displaying the ability to replace human doctors in the areas of generating hypotheses and evaluating the strength of those hypotheses (Friedman, 2014)

Question 6 asks: Do you currently use any aspect of advanced automation in your work environment? The results are as follows:

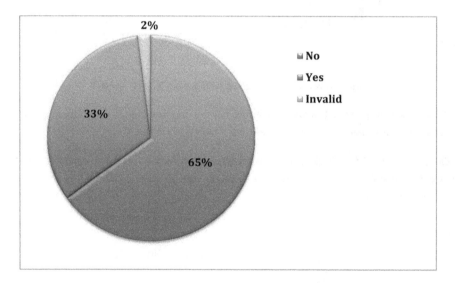

FIGURE 13: Is advanced automation used in your workplace?

With advanced automation expected to improve employment opportunities and be embraced as per the previous results, only 65% of respondents have actually currently implemented advanced automation in their current work environment. Two respondents choose to skip the question. This could point to the respondents not understanding the umbrella under which advanced automation could be determined within their own organization.

Question 7 asks: Do you believe this advanced automation has led to the replacement of any jobs in your work environment? The results are as follows:

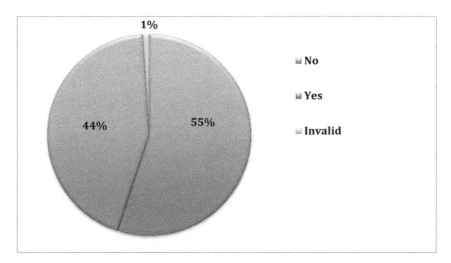

FIGURE 14: Has advanced automation replaced jobs in your workplace?

The majority of respondents believe advanced automation should be embraced, and that it would lead to an increase in job opportunities. However, 44% of respondents have also seen advanced automation replace existing jobs within their work environment. There was no follow up question to determine if the jobs have been completely removed, or the employment changed.

Question 8 asks: With the growth of advanced automation, do you fear for your own job in the future? The results are as follows:

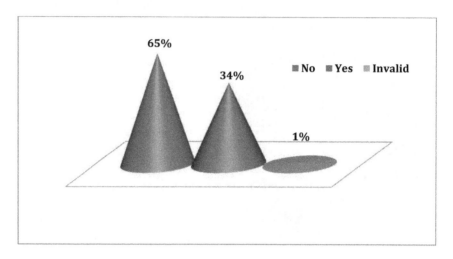

FIGURE 15: Do you fear for your own job?

Leading on from question 8, 44% of respondents have seen jobs in their current employment replaced by advanced automation, yet only 34% of respondents saw a need to fear for their jobs, with 14% of respondents believing advanced automation will have a negative impact on employment in the IT sector.

The majority, or 65%, did not perceive advanced automation as something that would impact their own employment, with one respondent skipping the question. The results shown correspond with a recent survey by online job recruitment company, *monster.ie*, who polled 3,800 workers about the possibility of their job been replaced by robots — 63% believed that their jobs would never be replaced by robots (Hunt, 2015). Hunt does not confirm what the respondent's jobs where for this survey.

From the survey, it is clear that the onset of advanced automation is upon us. It still has a long way to go; with only 35% currently implementing advanced automation in their work environment.

73% of IT professionals believe that its implementation will have a positive impact, and 66% of respondents feel that it should be fully embraced. 50% share the view that advanced automation will be complex enough within the next 20 years to replace skilled professionals, such as surgeons, pilots and accountants. Despite this opinion, a huge 85% of respondents still believe that this will have a positive effect on employment. It is therefore plausible to postulate that even though IT professionals are aware of the impending onset of advanced automation and the singularity, 72% still do not believe that this will impact employment in general. It can be deduced from this that not enough employment has been disrupted as of yet to pose a mainstream threat to current employees. It also leads us to believe that current IT workers believe that they bring enough knowledge and skill to their current jobs, and that they will not be impacted by such changes.

The survey demonstrates that users who deployed advanced automation in their work environment have seen more job losses than those who did not. The information gleaned from this data was taken from replies to the following two questions: 1) Do you believe advanced automation has led to the replacement of any jobs in your work environment?; 2) and do you currently use any aspect of advanced automation in your work environment?

From this, we were able to use the hypotheses that of the 33% of respondents who use advanced automation in their environment, 44% of them believe this has led to job removals in their work environment, whilst of the 65% who do not, 55% of them still believe that advanced automation has led to unemployment in their workplace, either through some outside factor or reducing demand due to advanced automation.

4.3.2 Cloud Services

This section addresses the data accumulated from questions 9-14.

Question 9 asks: Do you currently use cloud services in any aspect of your day-to-day job? The results are as follows:

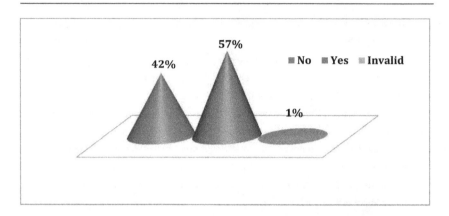

FIGURE 16: Do you currently use cloud service in your job?

57% of respondents currently use cloud servers in their day-to-day work environment, with a surprisingly high number of 42% saying they do not. It is possible that those who answered 'no' may have internal security policies that restrict them from revealing such details.

Question 10 asks: Do you intend to increase your use of cloud services or decrease your use over the next 12 months? The results are as follows:

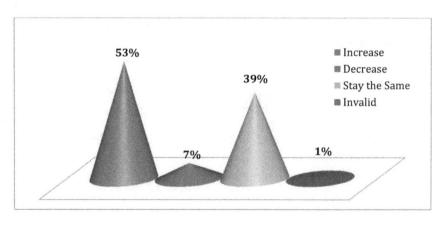

FIGURE 17: Do you plan to increase your use of cloud services?

53% of respondents are looking to increase their use of cloud services over the next 12 months, with 39% looking to stay the same, and 7% looking to decrease. One respondent choose not to answer. Gartner (2011) surveyed 2,014 CIOs, who represent more than $160 billion in CIO IT budgets, spanning 38 industries in 50 countries. The survey confirmed that over half the CIO's surveyed expected to operate the majority of their ICT requirements through cloud services over the next four years.

Question 11 asks: By moving to cloud based services, do you believe it reduces the amount of IT personnel needed in your company? The results are as follows:

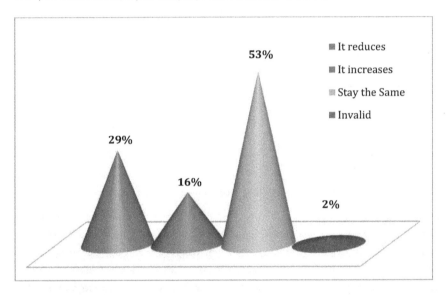

FIGURE 18: Does cloud reduce employment?

53% of respondents believe that the use of cloud services will have no impact on employment in their organization, with 29% supposing it will. Black et al., (2010) performed a study on IT departments implementing cloud services in North America and Europe. They surveyed 273 IT professionals, and 161 IT professionals in Europe. 52% would not support migration to cloud based services, due to the risk of job loss. Gartner believes there will be a decline in the ICT workforce as cloud computing matures (Feinman, 2010). The survey respondents disagree with this.

Question 12 asks: By moving some or all IT function to cloud services, do you find yourself more productive? The results are as follows:

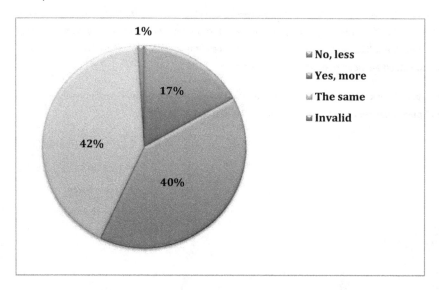

FIGURE 19: Does cloud make you more productive?

42% believe that the use of cloud services has no impact on their productivity, with 40% answering 'the same', and 17% conceding to being less productive thanks to cloud services. These findings disagree with a survey by Tata communications in which, according to their global study of 1,000 senior IT decision-makers in 2015, 69% reported increased productivity due to cloud services (Tata, 2015). This shows that current IT workers are aware of the increased amount of productivity expected from decision makers in their organisation for them to be more productivie with the increased use of cloud services. This might allow us to deduce that IT workers are disagreeing with this in order to safe guard their current level of work.

Question 13 asks: By moving to cloud services do you find yourself working more, outside your normal paid hours? The results are as follows:

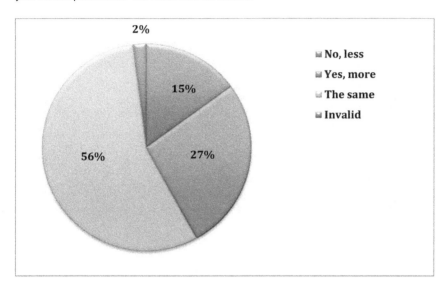

2%

15%

56%   27%

- No, less
- Yes, more
- The same
- Invalid

FIGURE 20: Are you working more unpaid hours due to the cloud?

The majority of respondents felt that they were working the same hours as always, even after switching to cloud services. By contrast, 27% felt they were working more hours outside their paid hours, and 15% felt they were working less. Two respondents choose not to answer. This would confirm that using cloud services can increase output but within the same worker hours as traditionally seen.

Question 14 asks: Do you trust the security of your data stored on a cloud platform? The results are as follows:

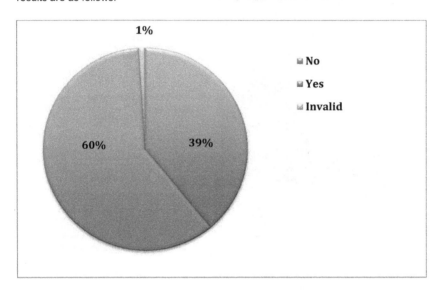

	Frequency	Percent	Valid Percent
No	43.00	38.74	39
Yes	67.00	60.36	60
Invalid	1.00	0.90	1
Total	111.00	100.00	100

FIGURE 21: Is your data secure on cloud platforms?

The survey recorded a strong level of trust in cloud providers from respondents' data. 60% believe their data was fully secure in the cloud, 39% disagreed, and one respondent choose not to answer.

The results show that cloud services are already dominant in the current work environment, with 63% using some form of cloud services in their day-to-day employment. This is only expected to grow, with 59% confirming that they plan to expand their usage of cloud services in the coming 12 months. According to 32% of respondents, this growth of cloud service usage will lead to a reduction in employment numbers. 40% of respondents are of the opinion that cloud services allow them to be more productive, with 43% seeing no increased output or productivity. 57% do not think that they are working more hours due to cloud services. Only 27% find that they now work more outside of normal paid hours.

There is a high level of trust in cloud-based services, with 61% seeing no issues or causes of concern with the security of their data on cloud platforms, and 39% demonstrating a level of distrust with this security level.

4.3.3 Data Centre

This section examines respondents' understanding and use of data centres through an analysis of questions 15-18. As the primary driver in cloud services and the growth of advanced automation, data centres provide the heartbeat of the IT sector. The knowledge of IT workers about these facilities will establish a clearer understanding of whether the physical underlying hardware structures in IT are becoming redundant or not, with IT moving towards being seen as a service and managed as any other disposal utility.

Question 15 asks: How would you describe a data centre?

A data centre is defined by Gartner as:

> ...the department in an enterprise that houses and maintains back-end information technology (IT) systems and data stores — its mainframes, servers and databases. In the days of large, centralized IT operations, this department and all the systems resided in one physical place, hence the name data center (Gartner, 2013).

As this was a text-based option, it allowed for a variety of replies based on the particpants' understanding of what such a building was used for. For reasons of clarity, this question was divided into three categories: 1) irrelevant; 2) intuitive knowledge; 3) and accurate knowledge. 48% showed an accurate knowledge, whilst 38% could be described as intuitive. 12% were inaccurate, with a large portion of respondents, 14, choosing not to give an answer. A word cloud (figure 22) highlights the key wording responses to this query as follows:

Answer Options	Response Percent	Response Count
Irrelevant	12.70%	7
Intuitive Knowledge	38.80%	40
Accurate Knowledge	48.50%	50
Answered question		97
Skipped question		14

FIGURE 22: Word cloud highlighting key words from text question 15

48% of respondents displayed either no knowledge, or just slightly intuitive knowledge, of what a data centre is. This would suggest that hardware is becoming more abstract in the minds of IT workers. Simson Garfinel from MIT states that 'the consequences of this shift are far reaching: one of the clearest is that today there's very little need for businesses to purchase a computer system other than PCs and laptops for employees' (Garfinel, 2011). Its use is now morphing into one of a utility, which can be used when needed and removed when individual jobs are completed. The focus of IT workers now seems to be on using technology, rather than displaying an understanding of how the underlying workings of the hardware that house and run that technology operate. This would account for a lack of understanding/ knowledge regarding how you would describe the functions of a data centre facility among IT workers who connect to servers housed in these facilities on a daily basis.

Question 16 asks: Do you currently use any data centre facilities for your own IT hardware? The results are as follows:

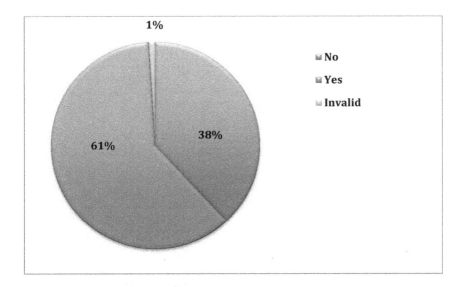

FIGURE 23: Do you house your hardware in a Data centre?

The majority of respondents house their own IT hardware in data centre facilities with 38% saying they did not. This corresponds with a 2014 survey from the Uptime Institute, which saw an 86% rise in budgets towards data centre colocation for their IT equipment (Uptime Institute, 2014). Server rooms and data centres across the country are running at much less than capacity, and they have become too powerful for their requirements — meaning less space is now required to run a similar level of IT services, as previously needed (Leavitt, 2009). □

Question 17 asks: Do you consider a data centre critical to your IT infrastructure? The results are as follows:

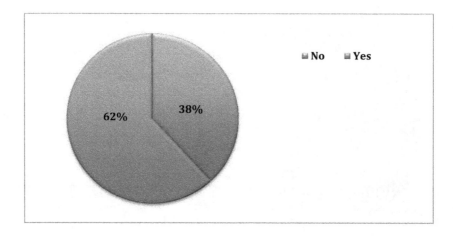

FIGURE 24: Is a data centre critical to your IT requirements?

Nearly two thirds of respondents confirmed that a data centre facility was critical to their IT infrastructure, with 38% saying it was not.

Question 18 asks: Are you concerned with which data centre is used to house your cloud services? The results are as follows:

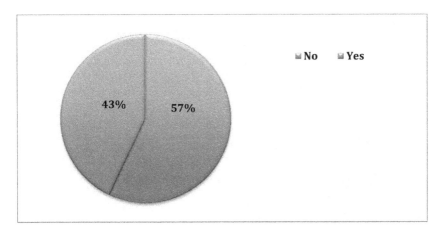

FIGURE 25: Is the data centre that contains your data a concern?

57% of respondents are not concerned with what data centre facility houses their data through the cloud services they use. 43% believed this to be of concern.

Data Centres are the lifeblood of the Internet, and the IT industry. Their importance is generally underestimated by layman users, and they are now becoming more abstract to IT workers who simply utilise the web-based tools hosted on cloud platforms to increase productivity and remove complexities for their end users. This lack of knowledge regarding the underlying facilities that house their data is conveyed in the high level of survey respondents (47%) who work in the IT sector, but could not display any knowledge of what the functions of a data centre are. This belief is further strengthened with 62% of respondents confirming they use a data centre facility to house their IT hardware, and 62% confirming a data centre would be termed as 'critical' to their IT infrastructure requirements. The actual physical data centre building, that house their 'critical' IT infrastructure is of no concern to 57% of respondents.

4.3.4 Employment in IT

This section explores the data collected from questions 19-21, which deals with the employment market in IT. Question 19 asks: Do you believe job opportunities in the IT sector will continue to increase or decrease? The results are as follows:

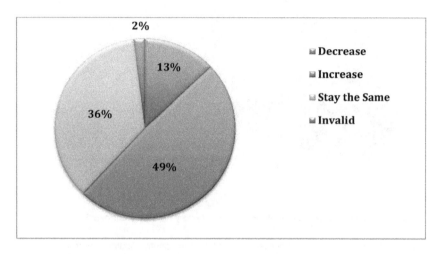

FIGURE 26: Will job opportunities increase or decrease?

Just half of the respondents, 49%, believe job opportunities will continue to increase in the IT sector. 13% are confident that they will decrease, while 36% believe that they will stay the same. According to the latest figures from U.S. Bureau of Labour Statistics (BLS), they expect IT jobs to grow by 22% by 2020 due to an increased demand for software developers in the Health IT and Mobile network sectors as shown in Figure 4 in chapter 2.

Question 20 asks: Do you believe education will be more important for job opportunities in the future? The results are as follows:

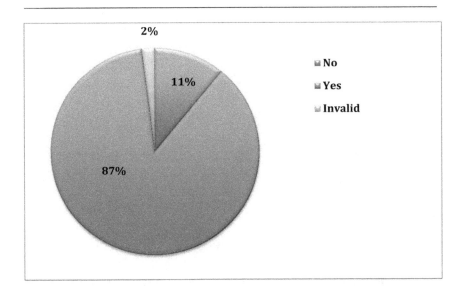

FIGURE 27: Is education important for future job opportunities?

An overwhelming majority of respondents consider education as being of vital importance for continued job opportunities in the future. Here, 87% answered 'yes', and only 11% said 'no'. Two respondents chose not to answer. Brynjolfsson and McAfee reinforce this idea by arguing that 'acquiring an excellent education is the best way to not be left behind as technology races ahead; motivated students and modern technologies are a formidable combination' (Brynjolfsson and McAfee, 2011).

Question 21 asks: Do you believe that knowing how to code/program is essential to future employment? The results are as follows:

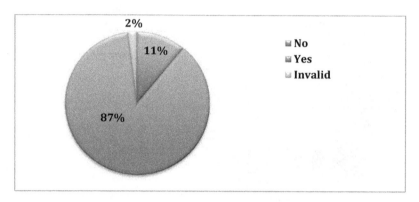

FIGURE 28: Do you believe that coding is important for future employment?

A near two-thirds majority of respondents believe knowing how to program or code is essential to future employment, with 87% answering 'yes', and 11% saying 'no', with 2 respondents choosing not to answer. As the respondents are IT workers this would be the expected response.

Question 22 asks: Do you know anyone with the relevant qualifications, who has found it hard to find employment in the IT sector? The results are as follows:

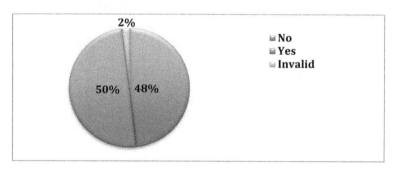

FIGURE 29: Are you aware of anyone in the IT sector who has found it hard to find employment?

Half of respondents knew suitably qualified candidates in the IT sector who found it challenging to find work, while 48% did not — thus tipping the scales slightly in favour of the 'yes' vote. Two respondents opted not to answer this question. This would imply that the two respondents could be potentially out of work at the time of the survey.

Half the respondents are confident that job opportunities will continue to increase in the IT sector. Education will be the driving factor in ensuring job opportunities with 89% confirming its importance. 65% also view the ability to code as a means of ensuring that these opportunities will present themselves. However, this is slightly contradicted by the 50% result of those who know of someone who struggled to find employment in the IT sector, despite having the relevant education and coding skills. This suggests that jobs in the IT sector are being displaced, and technological employment is having an effect on current available opportunities.

4.4 *Dediserve*: A Case Study

4.4.1 Introduction

Dediserve is a global infrastructure as a service provider with cloud platforms across Europe, the USA and Asia. Founded in Dublin, Ireland (2009), *dediserve* has endeavored to bring enterprise level architecture and hardware to a global market at a cost effective price, by driving the use of advanced automation on their platforms — providing both SMEs and Corporates with the ability to spin up servers around the globe via a single pane of glass in real time, and only pay for the resources when they need them. Traditionally, access to company's servers and IT would be locked down via a single location, usually the office for additional layers of security. Through the use of web portals, as well as IOS, Android and iPad applications users are now able to fully manage their complete IT infrastructure and architecture from no fixed location. This flexibility and use of advanced automation allows companies that use the service to vastly reduce the head count needed to traditionally monitor and respond to server issues, by removing the need to have an employee sitting at a single workstation 24/7 to respond to any potential issues that might arise. The survey conducted in this thesis demonstrates that 63% of respondents do not care where their cloud data is physically stored, showing functionality as now replacing the need to care about where users' data is physically stored. Yet 69% believe that knowledge of the location of their data centre is critical to their IT infrastructure.

Dediserve is now home to thousands of clients across the globe (Figure 30):

FIGURE 30: Geographical overview of *dediserve* customer base

4.4.2 Employment and Automation

Dediserve was founded with a single employee, with the first cloud platform launched in Dublin, Ireland. In the first year, 150 new customers where signed up, and no new employees were added. In year two, the company expanded to 600 customers, and two new employees were added to help build out systems and improve automation on the platforms. By year 2011, the employee numbers were at nine, with a customer base of 2000. As of 2015, the customer base has now exceeded 10,000 customers. However, the employee numbers remain at nine. This is due to large amounts of time and investment at the start of the growth curve, and ongoing every quarter of continuous investment in automation. Our survey respondents confirm this drive towards automation; with some 72% of respondents confirming that some form of automation is currently deployed in their workplace. This has allowed for the offloading of a huge amount of traditional manual invention and work to automated IT systems, which control our platforms and allow our customers to manage everything they need remotely. It is due to this that we now only need one support engineer for every 2000 clients, thus helping to reduce costs and increase growth and profit margins.

The following graph (Figure 31) represents the customer/staff ratio of *dediserve*. It currently indicates an upward growth of customers, whilst the level of staffing remains static:

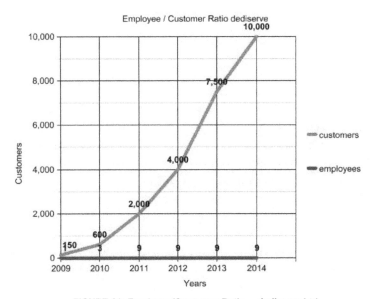

FIGURE 31: Employee/Customer Ratio – *dediserve* Ltd

The level of automation we use to run the business also extends beyond the technical function, with our accountancy functions completely outsourced. Through the use of *SaaS* (software as a service) tools such as *Xero*, all supplier/customers' invoices, as well as bank and credit card statements, are automatically recorded, categorised and managed via their online GUI. This is then managed completely by our remote accountant — removing the need for any in-house accountancy expertise.

With the investment into automation and the continued outsourcing of hardware to cloud providers such as *dediserve*, companies no longer need in-house IT administrators to manage their hardware. Through a combination of easy-to-use tools, even users with the most basic knowledge can now deploy servers and complex architecture. Combined with the ability to easily outsource server management and application deployment, the average SME, and even larger corporates, no longer require the need or use for a large in-house IT team. Cloud could actually be looked at as an automated form of outsourcing, devoid of the need to manage remote teams. As *dediserve* has shown, advanced automation is having a real world impact on the number of employees required to do the same amount of work as that which would have been needed previously. However, this current survey demonstrates that 86% of respondents believe the onset of advanced automation will provide a positive impact on their employment prospects, and 65% have no fears regarding their own employment.

4.5 Summary of Findings

This chapter presented a detailed analysis of the results of the data gathered by the research. The research question and hypotheses were used as a guide in the data analyses. The role of advanced automation and its impact was investigated from the perspective of current IT workers. It is clear from both the survey respondents, and the case study that advanced automation is now commonplace and continuing to grow.

Chapter 5 will discuss the findings that have arisen from this chapter, and the manner in which they correlate with the material reviewed in Chapter 2. This concluding chapter will investigate if the literature review corresponds to the current research findings of this present study. Subsequently, it will set out the necessary action steps required in response to these findings, thus providing future direction for research in this field.

5. Conclusions

5.1 Introduction

This thesis has investigated the impact of advanced automation and the cloud on employment within the IT sector. My analytic cue for such an undertaking has come from the increased public coverage on the subject, both in the media and academic circles. Of particular interest are the following: the paper by Frey and Osborne (2013), 'The Future of employment: How Susceptible are jobs to computerisation?', *The lights in the Tunnel* by Martin Ford, and *Race Against the Machine* by Erik Brynjolfsson and Andrew McAfee. Each work highlights the rise of advanced automation, and how this is going to have a severe impact on jobs and job opportunities due to technological employment.

It is clear from the literature review conducted in Chapter 2 that the age of advanced automation is now upon us. Here, it emerged that the manner in which society reacts to this new age defines its impact in future years.

It was determined, through the research strategy outlined in Chapter 3, that a pragmatic approach, combined with a survey of current IT workers situated on the front line of such changes, would provide insight into real world implementation of advanced automation. The resultant findings from this methodology were further substantiated in my case study on the IT company, *dediserve*, which has reduced its employment numbers through the use of advanced automation.

The outcome of this research was presented in Chapter 4, thus illuminating many of the obstacles and challenges that currently face both IT workers and industry. It also afforded a better understanding of the present knowledge base of those most affected by the changes in this landscape.

This thesis ultimately poses three fundamental questions which will be discussed below: 1) Will advanced automation impact employment?; 2) What occupations will see the impact?; and 3) What does our future with advanced automation look like?

5.2 Will Advanced Automation Impact Employment?

The findings of the survey conducted in Chapter 4 reveal that the vast majority of respondents believe that the evolution of advanced automation, and its impact on society, will have a primarily positive effect on both current and future job opportunities. This view is predominantly based on the historical evidence associated with previous technological advancements, which shows that an increased use of technology provides additional employment opportunities, rather than permanently removing those jobs.

My study shows that current IT workers imagine advanced automation as something to be embraced, thus suggesting that this will have a positive impact on employment opportunities. The results of my findings also indicate that people are evenly split on the level of intelligence and skill that advanced automation can attain in the next twenty years. 65% of respondents already use advanced automation in their employment, with the majority also witnessing job losses due to this development. McAfee (2011) concurs with these statistics, stating that 'new technologies are encroaching into human skills in a way that is completely unprecedented' (Rotman, 2013). Many middle-class jobs are now at the epicentere of this change, with even relatively high-skill work in education, medicine, and law affected. According to McAfee, 'the top and bottom are clearly getting farther apart'; while technology might be only one factor, albeit an 'underappreciated' one, it is likely to become increasingly significant.

The literature review compounds the general consensus among leading authors, such as Frey, Osborne, and Andrew McAfee, that unlike previous leaps we are now on the precipice of the singularity, which will have a more lasting and forceful impact than previously seen. While there is ongoing disagreement about the driving forces behind the persistently high unemployment rates, a number of scholars have pointed to computer-controlled equipment as a possible explanation for recent jobless growth (Brynjolfsson and McAfee, 2011; and Manning, 2013). It is also expected that, as cloud computing matures, it will reduce the ICT workforce (Feinman, 2010).

This thesis confirms that advanced automation will impact employment. While current workers may not be willing to acknowledge or accept that this will affect employment and employment opportunities, it has become clear that its influence and impact is real, and growing at a steadfast rate with 44% of firms having reduced their headcount since the financial crisis of 2008, and done so by means of automation (MGI, 2011). With the eventuality of the singularity, there is a clear indication that job growth, sustained employment and ongoing job creation, are going to pose formidable challenges for society and its people in the coming years.

5.3 Occupations Under Threat

A recent report from Deloitte and the University of Oxford states that high skilled jobs such as those in management, business, finance, as well as the services, are currently at risk from the increased use of advanced automation. The IT job sector is very much under threat according to a paper, just published in June 2015, entitled, 'Computer program fixes old code faster than expert engineers' as reported by Conner-Simons in MIT news in July 2015. Paper co-author Saman Amarasinghe states: 'we've found that Helium [the name of the software program they developed] can make updates in one day that would take human engineers upwards of three months' (Conner-Simons, 2015).

Knowledge-based jobs were traditionally looked upon as safe career choices — the years of study dedicated to becoming a lawyer, an architect, or an accountant, were, in theory, guaranteeing a lifetime of lucrative employment. That is no longer the case. Now, even doctors face the looming threat of possible obsolescence. Expert radiologists are routinely outperformed by pattern-recognition software, as are diagnosticians by simple computer questionnaires. In 2012 Silicon Valley investor, Vinod Khosla, predicted that algorithms and machines would replace 80% of doctors within a generation (Kholsa, 2012). This can be seen in the growth in complexity of IBM's super computer, Watson, which is already capable of storing far more medical information than doctors. Unlike humans, its decisions are all evidence-based, and free of cognitive biases and overconfidence. It is also capable of understanding natural language, generating hypotheses, evaluating the strength of those hypotheses, and learning — not just storing data, but finding meaning in it (Friedman, 2014).

In a recent survey of 2,571 executives in 36 economies, conducted by Grant Thornton (June 2015), over half (56%) of firms surveyed told Grant Thornton that they are either already automating business practices, or intend to do so over the next 12 months (Grant Thorton, 2015).

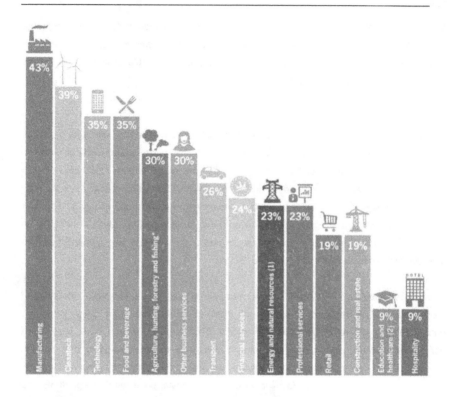

FIGURE 32: Percentage of businesses which expect automation to replace at least 5% of their workforce

In industry, 43% of manufacturing firms said they expect this to eventually replace at least 5% of their workforce. Cleantech was in second place on 39%, followed by the technology and food & beverage sectors on 35%. This suggests that currently low-paid repetitive or menial jobs are the most at risk. At the other end of the spectrum, just 9% of hospitality, education and healthcare firms expect 5% or more of workers to be replaced — showing those sectors as the most resilient to change due to automation (Grant Thorton, 2015). Other occupations under less risk are creative jobs, with Nesta's 'Creativity versus Robots' report finding highly creative roles are much less likely to be taken by robots, with 87% of these roles at low or no risk of automation in the UK (Nesta, 2015). The report ranked more than 500 professions, involving varying levels of creativity, to understand which jobs were under threat of automation. Artists, musicians, graphic designers, and computer game programmers are among the professions least likely to be replaced by robots over the next 20 years.

5.4 A Future with Advanced Automation

From the literature review, survey and case study, the general consensus is not concerned with if or when the singularity will happen. Results indicate that it is now clear that advanced automation is already causing job loss and obstacles to employment growth.

In order to avoid getting left behind, research has found that education is the key driver to staying relevant in today's job markets. Technological advancements now permeate wide segments of daily life, and are often completely unnoticed. Brynjolfsson and McAfee reinforce this idea by arguing that 'acquiring an excellent education is the best way to not be left behind as technology races ahead, motivated students and modern technologies are a formidable combination' (Brynjolfsson, McAfee, 2011). Dr Frank Shaw (foresight director at the Centre for Future Studies) confirms this: 'those professions that do not change will render themselves obsolete'; 'Those that are able to transform themselves – and I mean 'transform' – will thrive and prosper' (Meltzer, 2014).

A 2014 'Future of the Internet' survey saw 1,896 of respondents' replies categorised into either 'reasons to be hopeful', or 'reasons for concern' (Smith, Anderson, 2014) as follows:

Reasons to be hopeful:

- Advances in technology may displace certain types of work, but historically they have been a net creator of jobs.
- We will adapt to these changes by inventing entirely new types of work, and by taking advantage of uniquely human capabilities.
- Technology will free us from day-to-day drudgery, and allow us to define our relationship with "work" in a more positive and socially beneficial way.
- Ultimately, we as a society control our own destiny through the choices we make.

Reasons for concern:

- Impacts from automation have thus far impacted mostly blue-collar employment; the coming wave of innovation threatens to disrupt white-collar work as well.

- Certain highly-skilled workers will succeed in this new environment — but far more may be displaced into lower paying service industry jobs at best, or permanent unemployment at worst.
- Our educational system is not adequately preparing us for work of the future, and our political and economic institutions are poorly equipped to handle these hard choices.

The reasons for concern can be addressed through a restructuring of the current education system, which will allow for an easier path for traditional blue collar workers to up-skill to more advanced levels, in order to take advantage of the technical advancements and new employment opportunities that they are now being presented. As creativity will be the driving force in employment opportunities and security, a stronger emphasis needs to be placed on innovation through creativity within current educational bodies.

5.5 Limitations

The findings of this research have been limited to the responses of 111 IT professionals, and the case study of a single company aggressively employing automation in order to reduce employment.

It was not possible to canvass additional companies with regards to their implementation of advanced automation in their workplace. This data would have enhanced the hypothesis that companies are looking at technology in a bid to reduce employment, and help increase and drive profitability in their organisations.

The 111 respondents of the survey where all derived from the IT sector. However, the replies of each respondent were limited to unique individual experiences with regards to how advanced automation is affecting employment in their workplace. This would lead to most respondents providing personal opinion rather than hard data, which may only be available to senior management in each organisation.

5.6 Future Research Opportunities

It is hoped that this research can be used as a springboard for future expansion on the data needed from a larger subset of individuals in senior management roles across all employment sectors. By speaking directly with decision-makers who are making employment-effecting choices, through their implementation of advanced automation to replace people in their organisations, a better understanding of the driving forces associated with this change can be reached. Further investigation into the simplification of software products, which allow users to now bypass technical experience or knowledge, would also prove beneficial in assessing its impact on employment in the IT sector. Future research may also consider a geographically dispersed study population for cross-cultural comparisons.

5.7 Summary

In conclusion, it appears that the use of advanced automation and the cloud is steadily reducing the need or use for human workers. The business case within most organisations is now to drive the increased use of automation, and accelerate the use of cloud services, which in turn helps reduces head count, increase productivity and drive profit.

In order to ensure employment in the future, people will need to either follow a more creative route, or keep up to date with their technological knowledge through education, in a bid to enhance both their lives and those of future generations.

Education is the clear winner in avoiding a jobless future. This is evident from the data collated in this thesis, whereby the majority of respondents believe that education and the ability to code is of vital importance when looking for a job. This ever evolving landscape of employment, and the ability of people to adapt their skill sets, ensures that employment opportunities will continue to present themselves to the people that best adapt.

REFERENCES

ABC News 20/20 Special (2006) *Last Days on Earth*. Available at: https://www.youtube.com/watch?v=_2agUY3mF4I [Accessed 18 December 2014].

Adams, H. (1918/1946) *The education of Henry Adams: An Autobiography*. New York: Houghton Mifflin.

Anderson, T., Färe, R., Grosskopf, S., Inman, L., and Song, X. (2002) 'Further Ex-amination of Moore's Law with Data Envelopment Analysis', *Technological Forecasting and SocialChange*, 69 (5), pp. 465-477.

Aridas, T., and Pasquali, V. (2013) 'Unemployment Rates in Countries Around the World', *Global Finance Magazine*, 13 March. Available at: https://www.gfmag.com/global-data/economic-data/worlds-unemployment-ratescom [Accessed 4 December 2014].

Armstrong, S. (2012) 'How We're Predicting AI', *The Singularity Summit 2012*. Available at: http://fora.tv/2012/10/14/Stuart_Armstrong_How_Were_Predicting_AI [Accessed 19 December 2014].

Barden, L. (2008) 'Bobby Fischer', *The Guardian*, 19 January. Available at: http://www. theguardian.com/news/2008/jan/19/mainsection.obituaries [Acessed 6 January 2015].

Baum, S., Goertzel, B., and Goertzel, T. (2010) 'How long until human-level AI? Results from an expert assessment', *Technological Forecasting and Social Change*, 78 (1), pp. 185-195.

Becker, H. S. (1970) *Sociological Work: Method and Substance*. New Jersey: Transaction.

Berkeley, I. S. (1997) *What is Artificial Intelligence?* Available at: http://www.ucs. louisiana.edu/~isb9112/dept/phil341/wisai/WhatisAI.html [Accessed 14 December 2014].

Binet, A. (1905/1916) 'New methods for the diagnosis of the intellectual level of subnormals', *The Development of Intelligence in Children: The Binet-Simon Scale*, trans. by E.S. Kite. Baltimore: Williams & Wilkins.

Bhaskar, R. (2010) *Reclaiming Reality: A Critical Introduction to Contemporary Philosophy.* New York: Routledge. ☐

Black, L., Mandelbaum, J., Grover, I. and Marvi, Y. (2010) 'The Arrival of "Cloud Thinking". How and Why Cloud Computing Has Come of Age in Large Enterprises', *Management Insight Technologies.* Available at: http://www.computerworld.com.pt/media/2011/03/the_arrival_of_cloud_thinking.pdf [Accessed 14 December 2014].

Brynjolfsson, E., and McAfee, A. (2011) *Race against the machine: How the digital revolution is accelerating innovation, driving productivity, and irreversibly transforming employment and the economy.* Lexington, MA: Digital Frontier Press.

Brynjolfsson, E., and Jordan, J. (2010) 'Cloud computing and electricity: Beyond the utility model', *Communications of the ACM,* 53 (5), pp. 32-34.

Buckingham, W. (1962) 'Automation', *Annals of the American Academy of Political and Social Science,* 340, pp. 46-52.

Bureau of Labour Statistics (2014) *Employment, Hours, and Earnings from the Current Employment Statistics Survey (National) Data,* 4 December. Available at: http://data.bls.gov/pdq/SurveyOutputServlet [Accessed 4 December 2014].

Bryman, A., and Bell, E., (2011) *Business Research Methods.* 3rd edn. Cambridge: Oxford University Press.

Carcary, M., Doherty, E., and Conway, G. (2014) 'The Adoption of Cloud Computing by Irish SMEs — an Exploratory Study', The *Electronic Journal Information Systems* Evaluation, 17 (1), pp. 003-014).

Cerf, V. (2014) *When will robots take our jobs?.* Available at: http://businesstech.co.za/news/general/65062/when-will-robots-take-our-jobs/ [Accessed 2 July 2015].

Chalmers, D. J. (2010) 'The Singularity: A Philosophical Analysis', *Journal of Consciousness Studies, 17* (9-10), pp. 7-65.

Chen, N. C. and Lin, A. (2012) 'Cloud computing as an innovation: Perception, attitude, and adoption', *International Journal of Information Management*, 32(6), pp. 533-540.

Conner-Simons, A. (2015) *Computer program fixes old code faster than expert engineers.* Available at: http://newsoffice.mit.edu/2015/computer-program-fixes-old-code-faster-than-expert-engineers-0609 [Accessed 10 July 2015].

Creswell, J. (2002) *Research Design: Qualitative, Quantitative, and Mixed Methods Approaches*, 2nd Edn. Thousand Oaks, CA: Sage. ☐

Data Protection Commissioner (2015) *Data Protection Acts 1998 and 2003* [Ireland]. Available at: https://www.dataprotection.ie/viewdoc.asp?DocID=796 [Accessed 20 April 2015].

Durkee, D. (2010) 'Why Cloud Computing Will Never Be Free', *Communications of the ACM*, 53 (5), pp. 62-69.

Easton, G. (2010) 'Critical Realism in Case Study Research', *Industrial Marketing Management*, 39 (1), pp. 118-128.

Eddy, N. (2013) *Cloud Computing Reducing Costs, Improving Productivity.* Available at: http://www.eweek.com/small-business/cloud-computing-reducing-costsimproving-productivity.html [Accessed 24 June 2015].

Federal Reserve Board (2001) *Monetary Policy Report to the Congress.* Available at: http://www.federalreserve.gov/pubs/bulletin/2001/0801lead.pdf [Accessed 25 May 2015].

Feinman, J. (2010) *How to Keep Your Job From Disappearing Into the Cloud.* Available at: https://www.gartner.com/doc/1427424/job-disappearing-cloud
[Accessed 14 December 2014].

Flowers, P. (2009) *Research Philosophies — Importance and Relevance.* Available at: https://www.networkedcranfield.com/cell/Assigment%20Submissions/research%20philosophy%20-%20issue%201%20-%20final.pdf [Accessed 30 January 20145].

Ford, M. (2009) *The Lights in the Tunnel: Automation, Accelerating Technology and the Economy of the Future.* USA: Acculant.

Frey, C. B., and Osborne, M. A. (2013) 'The Future of Employment: How Susceptible Are Jobs To Computerisation?', *Oxford Martin Programme on the Impacts of Future Technology.* Available at: http://www.oxfordmartin.ox.ac.uk/ downloads/academic/The_Future _of_Employment.pdf [Accessed 17 September 2013].

Friedman, L. (2014) 'IBM's Watson Supercomputer may soon be the best doctor in the world', *Business Insider*, 22 April. Available at: http://www.businessinsider.com/ibms-watson-may-soon-be-the-best-doctor-in-the-world-2014-4?IR=T [Accessed 12 July 2015].

Friedman, T. (2004) *The World is Flat, The Globalised World in the Twenty-first century.* London: Penguin.

Fuentes-Nieva, Ricardo and Galasso, Nick (2014) 'Working for the Few, Political Capture and economic inequality', *Oxfam International.* London: Oxfam.

Gartner (2013) 'Data Center', *IT Glossary.* Available at: http://www.gartner.com/it-glossary/data-center [Accessed 2 July 2015].

Gartner (2006), *Gartner Says Eight of Ten Dollars Enterprises Spend on IT is "Dead Money"*, 9 October. Available at: http://www.gartner.com/newsroom/id/497088. [Accessed 25 May 2015].

Ghose, A. K., Majid, N. and Ernst, C (2008) *The Global Employment Challenge, International Labour Office.* Geneva: Academic Foundation.

Good, I. J. (1965) 'Speculations concerning the first ultra intelligent machine', in *Advances in Computers*, 6, ed. by F. L. Alt & M. Rubinoff, (pp. 31-88). New York: Academic Press.

Goodkind, N. (2013) *Robots on the Rise: Is Your Job at Risk?*, 4 February. Available at: http://finance.yahoo.com/blogs/daily-ticker/robots-rise-job-risk-140532110.html [Accessed 22 December 2014].

Gorle P., Clive, A., and Martech, M. (2011) 'The positive Impact of Industrial Robots on Employment', *International Federation of Robotics IFR*. Available at: http://www.ifr.org/ uploads/ media/Metra_Martech_Study_on_robots_02.pdf
[Accessed 14 December 2014].

Groves, R. F., Couper, M., Lepkowski, J., Singer, E. and Tourangeau, R. (2004) *Survey Methodology*, Wiley Series in Survey Methodology. New Jersey: John Wiley & Sons.

Guest, G., Namey, E. and Mitchell, M. L. (2013) *Collecting Qualitative Data, A Field Manual for Applied Research.* Thousand Oaks, CA: Sage.

Hawkins, J. and Blakeslee, S. (2005) *On Intelligence.* New York: Times Books.

Higbie, T. (2014) *This is probably a good time to say that I don't believe robots will eat all the jobs.* Available at: http://blog.pmarca.com/2014/06/13/this-is-probably-a-good-time-to-say-that-i-dont-believe-robots-will-eat-all-the-jobs/ [Accessed 13 January 2014].

Holbeche L., and Springett N. (2004) *In Search of Meaning in the Workplace.* Roffey Park Institute, Horsham, West Sussex. Available at: http://www4.rgu.ac.uk/ files/In%20Search %20of%20Meaning%20at%20Work.pdf [Accessed 4 December 2014].

Huether, D. (2006), 'The Case of the missing jobs', *Business Week*, 3 April. Available at: http://www.businessweeek.com/magazine/content/06_14/b3978116.htm
[Accessed 5 January 2015].

Hunt, G. (2015) *Robot overlords don't seem to scare us, majority think jobs are safe from automation.* Available at: https://www.siliconrepublic.com/careers/2015/ 04/20/robot-overlords-dont-seem-to-scare-us-majority-think-jobs-are-safe-from-automation [Accessed 20 May 2015].

IBM (1997) *Deep Blue, Transforming the world, Cultural impacts, the Team in their words*, 11 May. Available at: http://www-03.ibm.com/ibm/history/ibm100/ us/en/icons/deepblue/ [Accessed 6 January 2015].

IBM (2009) *20 Petaflop Sequoia Supercomputer,* 3 November. Available at: http://www-304.ibm.com/jct03004c/press/us/en/pressrelease/26599.wss [Accessed 9 January 2015].

IMF (2009) *World Economic Outlook: Crisis and Recovery, April 2009.* Available at: https://www.imf.org/external/pubs/ft/weo/2009/01/pdf/text.pdf [Accessed 25 May 2015].

International Labour Organisation (2013) *Global unemployment rising again but with significant differences across regions,* 22 January. Available at: http://ilo.org/global/about-the ilo/newsroom/news/WCMS_202320/lang--en/index.htm [Accessed 5 December 2014].

Kharif, O. (2013) ' Starbucks links coffee makers to web fueling $27B market', *Bloomberg Business,* 22 October. Available at: http://www.bloomberg. com/news/articles/2013-10-22/starbucks-links-coffee-makers-to-web-fueling-27b-market [Accessed 28 May 2015].

Kholsa, V. (2012) 'Machines will replace 80 percent of doctors', *Wired.co.uk,* 4 September. Available at: http://www.wired.co.uk/news/archive/2012-09/04/doctors-replaced-with-machines [Accessed 10 July 2015].

Kurzweil, R. (1990) The Age of Intelligent Machines. Cambridge: MIT Press.

Kurzweil, Ray (2005) *The Singularity is Near. When Humans Transcend Biology.* USA: Penguin.

Leavitt, N. (2009) 'Is Cloud Computing Really Ready for Prime Time?', *Computer,* 42, pp. 15-20.

Leontif, W., and Duchin, F. (1984) *The Impacts Of Automation On Employment, 1963-2000.* New York: Institute for Economic Analysis, New York University.

Lincoln, Y.S. and Guba, E.G. (2005), 'Paradigms and perspectives in contention', in *Handbook of Qualitative Research,* ed. by N. Denzin and Y. Lincoln, 2nd Edn., pp. 163-188). Thousand Oaks, CA: Sage.

Lucas, R. E. (1978), 'Unemployment Policy', *American Economic Review,* 68 (2), pp. 353-357. Available at: http://www.jstor.org/stable/1816720 [Accessed 12 December 2014].

Lunden, I. (2014) *Yahoo Lays off 400 employees in India*. Available at: http://techcrunch.com/2014/10/07/yahoo-lays-off-employees-in-india-reportedly-up-to-2000-affected/ [Accessed 12 January 2014].

Marston, S. and Li, Z. et al. (2011) *Cloud Computing — The Business Perspective*. Available at: http://www.sciencedirect.com/science/article/pii/S0167923610002393 [Accessed 14 December 2014].

McDonald, M. P. (2011) *Reimagining IT: The 2011 CIO Agenda*, Gartner. Available at: *https://www.gartner.com/doc/1524714/executive-summary-reimagining-it-cio* [Accessed 14 December 2014].

Meltzer, Tom (2014) 'Robot doctors, online lawyers and automated architects: the future of the professions?', *The Guardian*, 15 June. Available at: http://www.theguardian.com/technology/2014/jun/15/robot-doctors-online-lawyers-automated-architects-future-professions-jobs-technology [Accessed 10 July 2015].

Mingers, J. and Willcocks, L. P. (2005) Social Theory and Philosophy for Information Systems. London: Wiley.

Moore, G. E. (1965) 'Cramming more components onto integrated circuits', *Proceedings of the IEEE*, 86 (1). Available at: http://www.cs.utexas.edu/~fussell/courses/cs352h/papers/moore.pdf [Accessed 19 December 2014].

Moravec, H. P. (1999) *Robot: Mere Machine to Transcendent Mind*. New York: Oxford University Press.

Moksha, S. (2013) 'Theorizing Middle-Way Research Approach', *International Journal of Scientific Research and Reviews*, 2, pp. 22-56.

Neal, M. (2014) *Why Automation Today is Like Computers in the 1980s, Vice Media LLC*. Available at: http://motherboard.vice.com/read/why-automation-today-is-like-computers-in-the-1980s-video [Accessed 12 January 2014].
Nesbary, D. K. (2000) *Survey Research and the World Web*. London: Allyn & Bacon.

Nesta (2015) *Creativity vs Robots.* Available at: http://www.nesta.org.uk/news/future-shock/creativity-vs-robots [Accessed 5 July 2015].

Palmer, R. (1998) *The Sound of History: Songs and Social Comment.* London: Oxford University Press.

Pansiri, J. (2005) 'Pragmatism: a methodological approach to researching strategic alliances in tourism', *Tourism and Hospitality Planning & Development,* 2, pp. 191-206.

Peláez, A. L., and Kyriakou, D. (2008) 'Robots, Genes and Bytes: Technology Develop-ment and Social Changes Towards the Year 2020', *Technological Forecasting and Social Change,* 75 (8), pp. 1176-1201.

Punch, K. (2005) *Introduction to Social Research: Quantitative and Qualitative Approaches.* 2nd Edn. Thousand Oaks, CA: Sage.

Rai, S. (2014) *Jobs Cuts And Weeping Workers At IBM India.* Available at: http://www.forbes.com/sites/saritharai/2014/02/13/job-cuts-and-weeping-workers-at-ibm-india/ [Accessed 12 January 2014].

Rifkin, J. (2011) *The Third Industrial Revolution: How Lateral Power is Transforming Energy, The Economy and the World.* New York: Palgrave Macmillan.

Rotman, D. (2013) 'How Technology is Destroying Jobs', *MIT Technology Review.* Available at: http://www.technologyreview.com/featuredstory/515926/how-technol ogy-is-destroying-jobs/ [Accessed 5 January 2015].

Sandberg, A. (2009) 'An overview of models of technological singularity', *AGI-2010 Workshop: Roadmap and the Future of AI.* Available at: http://agi-conf.org/2010/wp-content/uploads/2009/06/agi10singmodels2.pdf. [Accessed 14 December 2014].

Saunders, M., Lewis, P., and Thornhill, A. (2009) Research Methods for Business Students, 5th Edn. Essex, England: Pearson Education.

Semuls, A. (2010) 'Robots are creating jobless recovery', *LA Times*, 7 December. Available at: http://latimesblogs.latimes.com/money_co/2010/12/mismatch-skills.html [Accessed 4 December 2014].

Scott, D. and Usher, R. (Eds.) (1996) *Understanding Educational Research*. London: Routledge.

Slaby, J. R. (2012) *Robotic Automation Emerges as a Threat to Traditional Low-Cost Outsourcing, HFS Research*. Available at: http://www.hfsresearch.com/Robotic-Automation-as-Threat-to-Traditional-Low-Cost-Outsourcing [Accessed 12 January 2014].

Smith, A., and Anderson, J. (2014) 'AI, Robotics, and the Future of Jobs'. *Pew Research Center*. Available at: http://www.pewinternet.org/2014/08/06/future-of-jobs/ [Accessed 25 May 2015].

Tharenou, P., Donohue, R., and Cooper, B., (2007) *Management Research Methods*. Cambridge: Cambridge University Press.

The Economist (2014) 'Coming to an office near you: The effect of today's technology on tomorrows will be immense and no country is ready for it', 18 January. Available at: http://www.economist.com/news/leaders/21594298-effect-todays-technolo gy-tomorrows-jobs-will-be-immenseand-no-country-ready[Accessed 20 December 2014].

The Bureau of Labor Statistics (1927) 'BLS Bulletin 439', *Handbook of Labor Statistics 1924-26*, p. 527.

Thibodeau, P. (2012) *IT Jobs will grow 22% through 2020, says U.S.* Available at: http://www.computerworld.com/article/2502348/it-management/it-jobs-will-grow-22--through-2020--says-u-s-.html?page=3 [Accessed 5 January 2015].

Thorton, G. (2015) *Global survey finds lower skill manufacturing jobs under threat as businesses embrace automation*. Available at: http://www.grant-thornton. co.uk/en/Media-Centre/News/2015/Global-survey-finds-lower-skill-manufacturing-jobs-under-threat-as-businesses-embrace-automation-/ [Accessed 10 July 2015].

Tovey, A. (2014) 'Ten million jobs at risk from advancing technology', *The Telegraph*, 10 November. Available at: http://www.telegraph.co.uk/finance/newsbysector/industry/11219688/Ten-million-jobs-at-risk-from-advancing-technology.html [Accessed 25 May 2015].

Turing, A. M. (1950) 'Computing Machinery and Intelligence', *Mind: A Quarterly Review of Psychology and Philosophy*, pp. 433-460.

Ulam, S. (1958) 'Tribute to John von Neumann', *Bulletin of the American Mathematical Society*. Available at: https://docs.google.com/file/d/0B-5-JeCa2Z7hb WcxTGsyU09H STg/edit?pli=1 [Accessed 18 December 2014].

Uptime Institute (2014) *Data center Industry Survey*. Available at: http://journal.uptime institute.com/2014-data-center-industry-survey/ [Accessed 23 June 2015].

Vinge, V. (1993) *The Coming Technological Singularity: How to Survive in the Post-Human Era*, Vernor Department of Mathematical Sciences, San Diego State University. Available at: https://www-rohan.sdsu.edu/faculty/vinge/misc/singularity. html [Accessed 18 December 2014].

Wallen, N. E. and Fraenkel, J. R. (2001) *Educational Research: A guide to the Process*. Mahwah, New Jersey: Lawrence Erlbaum.

Walsham, G. (2009) *Interpreting Information Systems in Organizations*. Available at: http://pustakalaya.org/eserv.php?pid=Pustakalaya:1663&dsID=GeoffWalsham2009_Interp retingInformationSystems.pdf [Accessed 30 January 2015].
Woirol, G. R. (1996), *The Technological Unemployment and Structural Unemployment Debates*. London: Greenwood Press.

Worstall, T. (2014) The machines are going to steal all our jobs!, 22 January. Available at: http://www.adamsmith.org/blog/economics/the-machines-are-   going-to-steal-all-our-jobs/ [Accessed 22 December 2014].

Wright, K. B. (2005) 'Researching Internet-Based Populations: Advantages and Disadvantages of Online Survey Research, Online Questionnaire Authoring Software

Packages, and Web Survey Services', *Journal of Computer-Mediated Communication*, 10 (3).

Yin, R. K. (1984) *Case Study Research: Design and Methods*. Newbury Park, CA: Sage.

Yudkowsky, E. S. (2007) *Three Major Sinulairty Schools*, Machine Intelligence Research Institute. Available at: http://www.yudkowsky.net/singularity/schools/ [Accessed 5 January 2015].

Zeilzer, D. (2013) *Robots taking jobs from every sector of the economy*, 4 February. Available at: http://moneymorning.com/2013/02/04/robots-taking-jobs-from-every-sector-of-the-economy/ [Accessed 20 December 2014].

APPENDICES

Appendix 1: Ethics Application

The image was deleted due to copyright reasons

Appendix 2: Information Page for Participants

PROJECT TITLE: Advanced Automation and the Cloud, its Impact on Employment

BACKGROUND OF RESEARCH: This questionnaire is part of a research project designed to understand current knowledge on the subject of 'advanced automation'. It examines the possible impact of the singularity, automation and the growth of cloud services on employment. As the particular emphasis of this study is on the IT sector, the questionnaire will be dispersed among current employees of this field.

One of the fundamental fears in the current global community is the exponential growth and continued sophistication of artificial intelligence. Of particular concern is the wide ranging impact that this growth will have on the world as we currently know it, and on the place of humans within that world in terms of employment and job opportunities.

This has become termed as 'the singularity' — the point in time when machines will become autonomous. It is this point, which will elevate machines and robotics from the current monotonous job operations to more high skilled areas.

This study looks into the possibility that this moment in time will lead to a huge reduction in both employment and job opportunities around the world, with some economists predicting up to a 50% job loss or more (Frey, Osborne 2013).

The survey will allow us to gain a more comprehensive understanding of the base knowledge of these issues from current employees in the IT sector. It will also provide insight into whether or not they believe these developments to have a direct or indirect impact on their future work prospects.

METHODS AND MEASUREMENTS: A survey will be used to gain a more inclusive comprehension of the real world impact of the growth of artificial intelligence in the IT sector.

Combined with the widespread use of cloud services, this survey will highlight the impact that growth in these services is having on current and future employment, through an analysis of the replies from people working in the IT sector today.

PARTICIPANTS: The participants will be chosen from both personal LinkedIn connections (1000+) and twitter followers (900 +), with approximately 95% working in the IT sector or in technical roles. Each contact on twitter and linkedin will be presented with a link to the online survey, once they click on this link it will open the survey for them to view the informed consent form as well as information sheet and also the option to proceed or exit without penalty.

I would expect at least 100 replies based from this data. This will ensure a broad selection of replies to each question.

DEBRIEFING ARRANGEMENTS: The debriefing page will immediately follow the last question on the survey. Participants will be thanked for their contribution and more information on the purpose of the study will be provided. The researcher's contact information will be listed and participants will be reminded to print a copy of the debriefing form for their records. Participants will also be given the option to withdraw their data at any point (once they have been fully informed on the intent and purpose of the study) without penalty.

There is no potential for conflict of interest at any stage. All data will be fully secured in accordance with guidelines set down by the data protection commission of Ireland.

Please note that you can opt-out of this research at any stage without penalty and without prejudice to your legal or ethical rights

Appendix 3: Informed Consent Form

LEAD RESEARCHERS: ☐Aidan Mc Carron

PROJECT TITLE: Advanced Automation and the Cloud, its Impact on Employment

BACKGROUND OF RESEARCH: This questionnaire is part of a research project designed to understand current knowledge on the subject of 'advanced automation'. It examines the possible impact of the singularity, automation and the growth of cloud services on employment. As the particular emphasis of this study is on the IT sector, the questionnaire will be dispersed among current employees of this field.

PROCEDURES OF THIS STUDY: This questionnaire should take no longer than fifteen minutes. It will be based on multiple choice answers from IT workers by observing their views on automation and cloud services, and its influence on employment in the IT sector.

PUBLICATION: Only general findings will be reported, without reference to identifiable individual results. Results of the research will form part of the dissertation in the Taught Masters Programme M.Sc. in Management of Information Systems in the School of Computer Science and Statistics, Trinity College Dublin, Ireland. The dissertation will be submitted to the School of Computer Science and Statistics on 1st September 2015.

DECLARATION:

- I am 18 years or older and am competent to provide consent. ☐
- I have read, or had read to me, a document providing information about this research and this consent form. I ☐have had the opportunity to ask questions and all my questions have been answered to my satisfaction. I☐understand the description of the research that is being provided to me. ☐
- I agree that my data is used for scientific purposes and I have no objection to having my data published in scientific☐publications in a way that does not reveal my identity. ☐
- I freely and voluntarily agree to be part of this research study, though without prejudice to my legal and ethical ☐rights. ☐

- In the extremely unlikely event that illicit activity is reported to me during the study or within a survey question response, I will be obliged to report it to appropriate authorities.
- I understand that I may refuse to answer any question, and that I may withdraw at any time without penalty. ☐
- As the survey is web based, participants with history of epilepsy should be aware.
- I understand that my participation is fully anonymous and that no personal details about me will be recorded. ☐
- I have received a copy of this agreement. ☐

PARTICIPANT'S NAME:

PARTICIPANT'S SIGNATURE: < provided by digital signature>

Date: ☐

Statement of investigator's responsibility: I have explained the nature and purpose of this research study, the procedures to be undertaken and any risks that may be involved. I have offered to answer any questions and fully answered such questions. I believe that the participant understands my explanation and has freely given informed consent. ☐

INVESTIGATOR'S SIGNATURE:

Date: ☐

Appendix 4: Survey

You are invited to participate in this research project 'Advanced Automation and the Cloud, its Impact on Employment'.
Your participation is voluntary. Before you decide to take part in this survey, please read the information sheet below to find out the reasons behind the research, and your role in the process.

==

I am an MSc student on the Management of Information Systems course at Trinity College, Dublin. I am working on a dissertation unde the supervision of assistant Professor Diana Wilson. The primary aim of my research is to asses the level of knowledge in the IT sector regarding advanced automation and the cloud and its Impact on Employment

My work also examines the influence of advanced automation and cloud services on current and future employment within the IT secto

I have no conflict of interest with regard to the research topic and participants, either individually or any other level (employment or university).
All survey data collected will be strong password protected and will be permanently deleted on conclusion of the study October 2015.

There are 22 questions on this survey, it will take approximately 10 - 15 minutes to fully complete.

- Your participation is voluntary.

- Each participant may take the survey once.

- All data will be treated with full confidentiality and all contributors will remain anonymous if published.

- On request, an electronic version of this research will be available after September 2nd, 2015.

- You must be 18 years or older and competent to supply consent.

- You can opt-out at anytime by simply clicking the exit link on the top right hand corner at anytime without penalty.

==

Participation is confidential, and any information which I may obtain from you during the survey responses will be stored or published o a strictly anonymous basis. Third party anonymity in analysis, publication and presentation of resulting data and findings will also be in place

If you have any questions about this survey or the research study in general, please do not hesitate to contact me on ▇▇▇▇▇▇▇

LEAD RESEARCHER: Aidan Mc Carron

PROJECT TITLE: Advanced Automation and the Cloud, its Impact on Employment

BACKGROUND OF RESEARCH: This questionnaire is part of a research project designed to understand current knowledge on the subject of 'advanced automation'. It examines the possible impact of the singularity, automation and the growth of cloud services on employment. As the particular emphasis of this study is on the IT sector, the questionnaire will be dispersed among current employees of this field.

PROCEDURES OF THIS STUDY: This questionnaire should take no longer than fifteen minutes. It will be based on multiple choice answers from IT workers by observing their views on automation and cloud services, and its influence on employment in the IT sector.

PUBLICATION: Only general findings will be reported, without reference to identifiable individual results. Results of the research will form part of the dissertation in the Taught Masters Programme M.Sc. in Management of Information Systems in the School of Computer Science and Statistics, Trinity College Dublin, Ireland. The dissertation will be submitted to the School of Computer Science and Statistics on 1st September 2015.

DECLARATION:

· I am 18 years or older and am competent to provide consent.
· I have read, or had read to me, a document providing information about this research and this consent form. I have had the opportunity to ask questions and all my questions have been answered to my satisfaction. I understand the description of the research that is being provided to me.
· I agree that my data is used for scientific purposes and I have no objection to having my data published in scientific publications in a way that does not reveal my identity.
· I freely and voluntarily agree to be part of this research study, though without prejudice to my legal and ethical rights.
· In the extremely unlikely event that illicit activity is reported to me during the study or within a survey question response, I will be obliged to report it to appropriate authorities.
· I understand that I may refuse to answer any question, and that I may withdraw at any time without penalty by clicking the exit button on the top right hand corner.
· I understand that my participation is fully anonymous and that no personal details about me will be recorded.
· As the survey is web based, participants with history of epilepsy should be aware.
· I have received a copy of this agreement.

Statement of investigator's responsibility: I have explained the nature and purpose of this research study, the procedures to be undertaken and any risk that may be involved. I have offered to answer any questions and fully answered such questions. I believe that the participant understands my explanation and has freely given informed consent.

RESEARCHERS CONTACT DETAILS: Aidan Mc Carron, amccarr@tcd.ie

1. I agree to the above statements and wish to proceed to the survey.

◯ Yes
◯ No

The Impact of Advanced Automation and the Cloud on Employment
September 2015

Each question is optional. Feel free to omit a response to any question; however the researcher would be grateful if all questions are responded to.

2. Do you believe advanced automation will have a positive or negative impact on employment overall?

○ Positive

○ Negative

3. Do you believe advanced automation should be feared or embraced?

○ It should be feared

○ It should be embraced

○ Neither

4. Do you believe advanced automation will have a positive or negative impact on employment in the IT sector?

○ Positive

○ Negative

5. Do you believe advanced automation will become intelligent enough to fully replace high skilled jobs in the next 10 to 20 years such as surgery, accountancy or flight control?

○ Yes

○ No

6. Do you currently use any aspect of advanced automation in your work environment?

○ Yes

○ No

7. Do you believe this advanced automation has led to the replacement of any jobs in your work environment?

○ Yes

○ No

8. With the growth of advanced automation, do you fear for your own job in the future?

○ Yes

○ No

Each question is optional. Feel free to omit a response to any question; however the researcher would be grateful if all questions are responded to.

9. Do you currently use cloud services in any aspect of your day-to-day job?

◯ Yes

◯ No

10. Do you intend to increase your use of cloud services or decrease your use over the next 12 months?

◯ Increase

◯ Decrease

◯ Stay the Same

11. By moving to cloud based services do you believe it reduces the amount of IT personnel needed in your company?

◯ It reduces

◯ It increases

◯ Stay the Same

12. By moving some or all IT function to cloud services, do you find yourself more productive?

◯ Yes, more

◯ No, less

◯ The Same

13. By moving to cloud services, do you find yourself working more, outside your normal paid hours?

◯ Yes, more

◯ No, less

◯ The Same

14. Do you trust the security of your data stored on a cloud platform?

◯ Yes

◯ No

Each question is optional. Feel free to omit a response to any question; however the researcher would be grateful if all questions are responded to.

15. How would you describe a data centre?

16. Do you currently use any data centre facilities for your own IT hardware?

◯ Yes

◯ No

17. Do you consider a data centre critical to your IT infrastructure?

◯ Yes

◯ No

18. Are you concerned which data centre is used to house your cloud services?

◯ Yes

◯ No

Each question is optional. Feel free to omit a response to any question; however the researcher would be grateful if all questions are responded to.

19. Do you believe job opportunities in the IT sector will continue to increase or decrease?

◯ Increase

◯ Decrease

◯ Stay the Same

20. Do you believe education will be more important for job opportunities in the future?

◯ Yes

◯ No

21. Do you believe knowing how to code/program is essential to future employment?

◯ Yes

◯ No

22. Do you know anyone with the relevant qualifications who has found it hard to find employment in the IT sector?

◯ Yes

◯ No

YOUR KNOWLEDGE HAS VALUE

- We will publish your bachelor's and
  master's thesis, essays and papers

- Your own eBook and book -
  sold worldwide in all relevant shops

- Earn money with each sale

Upload your text at www.GRIN.com
and publish for free

www.ingramcontent.com/pod-product-compliance
Lightning Source LLC
La Vergne TN
LVHW092343060326
832902LV00008B/777